Managing Operations

Titles in the Institute of Management Series

Managing Operations

Bob Johnson

*Published in association with
the Institute of Management*

the Institute
of Management

FOUNDATION

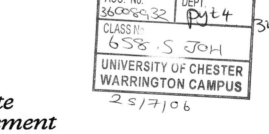
BUTTERWORTH
HEINEMANN

OXFORD   BOSTON   JOHANNESBURG   MELBOURNE   NEW DELHI   SINGAPORE

Butterworth-Heinemann
Linacre House, Jordan Hill, Oxford OX2 8DP
225 Wildwood Avenue, Woburn, MA 01801-2041
A division of Reed Educational and Professional Publishing Ltd

℟ A member of the Reed Elsevier plc group

First published 1998
Transferred to digital printing 2004
© Reed Educational and Professional Publishing Ltd 1998

British Library Cataloguing in Publication Data
Johnson, Bob
    Managing operations. – (IM Certificate in management
    series)
    I. Production management
    I. Title   II. Institute of Management
    658.5

ISBN 0 7506 3809 5

Composition by Genesis Typesetting, Rochester, Kent

Contents

Series adviser's preface

This book is one of a series designed for people wanting to develop their capabilities as managers. You might think that there isn't anything very new in that. In one way you would be right. The fact that very many people want to learn to become better managers is not new, and for many years a wide range of approaches to such learning and development has been available. These have included courses leading to formal qualifications, organizationally-based management development programmes and a whole variety of self-study materials. A copious literature, extending from academic textbooks to sometimes idiosyncratic prescriptions from successful managers and consultants, has existed to aid – or perhaps confuse – the potential seeker after managerial truth and enlightenment.

So what is new about this series? In fact, a great deal – marking in some ways a revolution in our thinking both about the art of managing and also the process of developing managers.

Where did it all begin? Like most revolutions, although there may be a single, identifiable act that precipitated the uprising, the roots of discontent are many and long-established. The debate about the performance of British managers, the way managers are educated and trained, and the extent to which shortcomings in both these areas have contributed to our economic decline, has been running for several decades.

Until recently, this debate had been marked by periods of frenetic activity – stimulated by some report or enquiry and perhaps ending in some new initiatives or policy changes – followed by relatively long periods of comparative calm. But the underlying causes for concern persisted. Basically, the majority of managers in the UK appeared to have little or no training for their role, certainly far less than their counterparts in our major competitor nations. And there was concern about the nature, style and appropriateness of the management education and training that was available.

The catalyst for this latest revolution came in late 1986 and early 1987, when three major reports reopened the whole issue. The 1987 reports were *The Making of British Managers* by John Constable and Roger McCormick, carried out for the British Institute of Management and the CBI, and *The Making of*

Managers by Charles Handy, carried out for the (then) Manpower Services Commission, National Economic Development Office and British Institute of Management. The 1986 report, which often receives less recognition than it deserves as a key contribution to the recent changes, was *Management Training: context and process* by Iain Mangham and Mick Silver, carried out for the Economic and Social Research Council and the Department of Trade and Industry. This is not the place to review in detail what the reports said. Indeed, they and their consequences are discussed in several places in this series of books. But essentially they confirmed that:

- British managers were undertrained by comparison with their counterparts internationally.
- The majority of employers invested far too little in training and developing their managers.
- Many employers found it difficult to specify with any degree of detail just what it was that they required successful managers to be able to do.

The Constable/McCormick and Handy reports advanced various recommendations for addressing these problems, involving an expansion of management education and development, a reformed structure of qualifications and a commitment from employers to a code of practice for management development. While this analysis was not new, and had echoes of much that had been said in earlier debates, this time a few leading individuals determined that the response should be both radical and permanent. The response was coordinated by the newly-established Council for Management Education and Development (now the National Forum for Management Education and Development (NFMED)) under the energetic and visionary leadership of Bob (now Sir Bob) Reid, formerly of Shell UK and the British Railways Board.

Under the umbrella of NFMED a series of employer-led working parties tackled the problem of defining what it was that managers should be able to do, and how this differed for people at different levels in their organizations; how this satisfactory ability to perform might be verified; and how an appropriate structure of management qualifications could be put in place. This work drew upon the methods used to specify vocational standards in industry and commerce, and led to the development and introduction of competence-based management standards and qualifications. In this context, competence is defined as the ability to perform the activities within an occupation or function to the standards expected in employment.

It is this competence-based approach that is new in our thinking about the manager's capabilities. It is also what is new about this series of books, in that they are designed to support both this new structure of management standards, and of development activities based on it. The series was originally commissioned to support the Institute of Management's Certificate and

Diploma qualifications, which were one of the first to be based on the new standards. However, these books are equally appropriate to any university, college or indeed company course leading to a certificate in management or diploma in management studies.

The standards were specified through an extensive process of consultation with a large number of managers in organizations of many different types and sizes. They are therefore employment-based and employer-supported. And they fill the gap that Mangham and Silver identified – now we do have a language to describe what it is employers want their managers to be able to do – at least in part.

If you are engaged in any form of management development leading to a certificate or diploma qualification conforming to the national management standards, then you are probably already familiar with most of the key ideas on which the standards are based. To achieve their key purpose, which is defined as achieving the organization's objectives and continuously improving its performance, managers need to perform four key roles: managing operations, managing finance, managing people and managing information. Each of these key roles has a sub-structure of units and elements, each with associated performance and assessment criteria.

The reason for the qualification 'in part' is that organizations are different, and jobs within them are different. Thus the generic management standards probably do not cover all the management competences that you may need to possess in your job. There are almost certainly additional things, specific to your own situation in your own organization, that you need to be able to do. The standards are necessary, but almost certainly not sufficient. Only you, in discussion with your boss, will be able to decide what other capabilities you need to possess. But the standards are a place to start, a basis on which to build. Once you have demonstrated your proficiency against the standards, it will stand you in good stead as you progress through your organization, or change jobs.

So how do the new standards change the process by which you develop yourself as a manager? They change the process of development, or of gaining a management qualification, quite a lot. It is no longer a question of acquiring information and facts, perhaps by being 'taught' in some classroom environment, and then being tested to see what you can recall. It involves demonstrating, in a quite specific way, that you can do certain things to a particular standard of performance. And because of this, it puts a much greater onus on you to manage your own development, to decide how you can demonstrate any particular competence, what evidence you need to present, and how you can collect it. Of course, there will always be people to advise and guide you in this, if you need help.

But there is another dimension, and it is to this that this series of books is addressed. While the standards stress ability to perform, they do not ignore the traditional knowledge base that has been associated with management studies.

Rather, they set this in a different context. The standards are supported by 'underpinning knowledge and understanding', which has three components:

- Purpose and context, which is knowledge and understanding of the manager's objectives, and of the relevant organizational and environmental influences, opportunities and values.
- Principles and methods, which is knowledge and understanding of the theories, models, principles, methods and techniques that provide the basis of competent managerial performance.
- Data, which is knowledge and understanding of specific facts likely to be important to meeting the standards.

Possession of the relevant knowledge and understanding underpinning the standards is needed to support competent managerial performance as specified in the standards. It also has an important role in supporting the transferability of management capabilities. It helps to ensure that you have done more than learned 'the way we do things around here' in your own organization. It indicates a recognition of the wider things which underpin competence, and that you will be able to change jobs or organizations and still be able to perform effectively.

These books cover the knowledge and understanding underpinning the management standards, most specifically in the category of principles and methods. But their coverage is not limited to the minimum required by the standards, and extends in both depth and breadth in many areas. The authors have tried to approach these underlying principles and methods in a practical way. They use many short cases and examples which we hope will demonstrate how, in practice, the principles and methods, and knowledge of purpose and context plus data, support the ability to perform as required by the management standards. In particular we hope that this type of presentation will enable you to identify and learn from similar examples in your own managerial work.

You will already have noticed that one consequence of this new focus on the standards is that the traditional 'functional' packages of knowledge and theory do not appear. The standard textbook titles such as 'quantitative methods', 'production management', 'organizational behaviour', etc. disappear. Instead, principles and methods have been collected together in clusters that more closely match the key roles within the standards. You will also find a small degree of overlap in some of the volumes, because some principles and methods support several of the individual units within the standards. We hope you will find this useful reinforcement.

Having described the positive aspects of standards-based management development, it would be wrong to finish without a few cautionary remarks.

The developments described above may seem simple, logical and uncontroversial. It did not always seem that way in the years of work which led up to the introduction of the standards. To revert to the revolution analogy, the process has been marked by ideological conflict and battles over sovereignty and territory. It has sometimes been unclear which side various parties are on – and indeed how many sides there are! The revolution, if well advanced, is not at an end. Guerrilla warfare continues in parts of the territory.

Perhaps the best way of describing this is to say that, while competence-based standards are widely recognized as at least a major part of the answer to improving managerial performance, they are not the whole answer. There is still some debate about the way competences are defined, and whether those in the standards are the most appropriate on which to base assessment of managerial performance. There are other models of management competences than those in the standards.

There is also a danger in separating management performance into a set of discrete components. The whole is, and needs to be, more than the sum of the parts. Just like bowling an off-break in cricket, practising a golf swing or forehand drive in tennis, you have to combine all the separate movements into a smooth, flowing action. How you combine the competences, and build on them, will mark your own individual style as a manager.

We should also be careful not to see the standards as set in stone. They determine what today's managers need to be able to do. As the arena in which managers operate changes, then so will the standards. The lesson for all of us as managers is that we need to go on learning and developing, acquiring new skills or refining existing ones. Obtaining your certificate or diploma is like passing a mile post, not crossing the finishing line.

All the changes and developments of recent years have brought management qualifications, and the processes by which they are gained, much closer to your job as a manager. We hope these books support this process by providing bridges between your own experience and the underlying principles and methods which will help you to demonstrate your competence. Already, there is a lot of evidence that managers enjoy the challenge of demonstrating competence, and find immediate benefits in their jobs from the programmes based on these new-style qualifications. We hope you do too. Good luck in your career development.

Paul Jervis

Introduction: what is operations management?

Definition

Operations management is not merely an alternative description for those functions which are otherwise known as production management or manufacturing management. Nevertheless, if you are employed in one of those functions you will find that many of the techniques used in operations management have a considerable contribution to make to them.

Instead, the scope of operations management is much broader, making it relevant to just about every function in any sphere of activity – from personnel to accounting, from government service to charities. Chapter 1 describes the way operations management takes place in a wide range of commercial, industrial and not-for-profit activities.

The following definition establishes the scope of operations management:

> The activities carried out by an organization to provide the service to customers or clients which is its basic reason for existing.

This definition is so broad that it will be helpful to draw out its key elements and implications.

Transformation and added value

It is generally accepted that organizations exist to create added value for customers by transforming inputs into outputs. This topic is developed further in Chapter 1. For the moment a few examples will clarify the point:

- Manufacturing businesses transform raw materials into finished goods.
- Haulage businesses transform freight by moving it from its point of manufacture or import to where the customer wants it.
- Charities transform public goodwill into potential aid.
- Publishers transform authors' ideas into instruction or entertainment for readers.

Transformation adds value in many forms. It may result in outputs which offer convenience, availability, ease of access or which customers cannot create for themselves. In Chapter 2 I explain how organizations decide the outputs and value they will offer through the strategic planning process, and the customers they will seek to satisfy. We also describe the impact of those decisions on operations managers.

Effectiveness, efficiency and responsiveness

The transformation process costs money. Customers will only pay a limited amount for added value: if the price exceeds the value, they will look elsewhere or go without. Consequently, as Chapter 3 explains, it is important for operations managers to ensure that the operations for which they are responsible are:

- effective – meeting customer needs, on time, every time
- efficient – keeping costs and inputs to a minimum
- responsive – adapting to changes in the external environment, competition and customer requirements.

Further chapters in this book address aspects of these three essentials. Chapter 5 considers the need to match quality to customer expectations. Chapter 7 explores ways of measuring performance, whilst Chapters 8 and 9 focus on identifying and correcting performance shortfall.

Customers

Customers were traditionally seen as coming at the end of the production chain and contact with them was limited to sales, marketing and accounts staff. This is no longer the case. As Chapter 4 points out, organizations are increasingly recognizing the importance of internal customers, which radically alters the role of operations managers. In order to meet the requirements of internal customers, operations managers are responsible for:

- identifying their needs (Chapter 4)
- meeting their expectations (Chapter 5)
- matching or exceeding the competition (Chapter 8).

These chapters introduce ideas drawn from total quality management, marketing, and organization development.

Managing resources

This is the title of Chapter 3, but the theme underlies the content of other chapters as well. The resources used in transforming inputs into outputs are made up of raw materials and components, equipment or fixed assets and people. Chapter 3 explores the ways of adapting the availability of resources to customer demand. Chapter 6 examines the importance of maintaining a healthy and safe working environment, whilst the focus of Chapter 10 is people – bosses, peers and subordinates.

The focus of the book can be summarized by stating that managing operations involves:

- ensuring that operational objectives are consistent with corporate goals
- identifying and satisfying the needs of customers (both internal and external)
- achieving efficient and cost-effective outputs
- monitoring and improving performance
- making optimum use of resources.

You may be wondering where people fit into this summary. The answer is that they are too important to be dismissed with a single phrase.

At various points in this book I shall suggest that:

- you will need the support of others to identify, rectify and implement operational improvements
- your staff are essential to performance
- your manager may be your only source of strategic direction
- change cannot be imposed, it must be welcomed
- your staff are a key resource
- the nature of the operation should reflect your staff's capability
- the extent to which you can improve your operation depends on the extent to which you involve and develop your staff.

By the end of the book you should be able to answer the following questions:

- What inputs and resources do you use?
- What transformations are you responsible for?

- Who are your customers? What are their requirements and expectations?
- How does your operation contribute to the achievement of your organization's goals?
- What actions could you take to improve quality?
- Why are health and safety issues important to you?
- How can you measure performance?
- What should you do with performance data?
- When is operational improvement necessary?
- What are the risks of improvement and change?
- Whose support do you depend on?
- How can you increase their contribution and co-operation?

Finally, you should recognize that all managers have an operations management role, regardless of the inputs and resources they use, the transformation and outputs for which they are responsible, their titles, functions or the type of organization which employs them.

1 Operations: the engine of the business

Four managers were debating the relative importance of the functions which they represented.

'A business can't do anything without finance', argued the accountant. 'Without money, there'd be no resources. If we didn't make a profit, we'd go bust. The finance function has a vital job to do. You depend on us to raise the money you need, to make sure everything you do is cost-effective and that you make enough profit for the business to survive'.

'That's all very well', replied the marketing manager, 'but finance doesn't make money. You just borrow it from somebody else, then stop us wasting it. The biggest contribution you make is to say 'No, we can't afford it'. It's marketing that's most important. We're the people who find out what customers want, make sure our products and services meet their needs, tell customers about them and persuade them to buy. You may count the money, but we're the ones who make it'.

'Now hang on', interjected the personnel officer. 'You're both missing the point. Our business depends on people. Whether they're accountants, administrators, sales staff or shop-floor workers, someone needs to recruit them, pay them, deal with the unions, handle their complaints, train them and keep them happy. Of course, we work with line managers to do a lot of that, but don't forget that our staff are our most important resource. And without the personnel function they just wouldn't be there'.

The supervisor from the production line felt a bit overawed by all this. Of course, he saw the accounts for the factory – he and his colleagues reviewed them with the Production Manager once a month. And he knew that finished goods from the line were packed and sent to customers. He'd been involved with personnel when he'd been promoted to supervisor – and it was obvious that someone must prepare the payroll, otherwise nobody would get paid! But surely finance, marketing and personnel were all support functions – there to help him and his production colleagues get on with the real work: making the things that customers paid for. He tried to put his thoughts into words.

'You marketing people talk about "adding value". Well, it seems to me that it's production that does that more than anyone else. We take raw materials and subassemblies, process them and put them together to make the finished goods that customers want. We transform bits that are useless in their original state into products that serve a useful purpose. Without us, marketing would have nothing to sell, finance would have nothing to count and there'd be no need for personnel'.

This debate is typical of discussions which take place regularly in organizations. As you would expect, all the speakers are attempting to justify their own function as the one on which the business depends. As you would also expect, in making their cases, each speaker is making selective use of points in their favour – and conveniently ignoring others!

The four functions represented in the debate – finance, marketing, personnel, operations – are commonly recognized as the core activities which make up the work of any organization. That organization may be:

- a retail business
- a manufacturing business
- offering a service such as dry-cleaning, training courses or vehicle maintenance
- a charity
- a hospital
- a government department
- a local council
- a school or college.

In all cases, the organization will be dependent on the work of all four functions, as will become evident from the descriptions below.

FINANCE

Many managers have difficulty with the principles of finance – and even more with the conventions of accounting! That does not change the fact that the finance function, as our accountant mentioned in the debate, does play a vital role in business. There are two parts to the role. The first is the management of money as a resource. All organizations require resources to conduct their business. These are likely to be made up of materials, labour, premises and equipment. But all these resources need to be paid for. At start-up and during periods of expansion, the organization is unlikely to have enough money to pay for the resources it needs. It will gain access to that money through borrowing or through issuing shares.

Most organizations carry at least some burden of debt. That raises the obligation to ensure that lenders' or shareholders' money is used carefully. Which brings us to the second part of the finance role – to monitor income and expenditure. Financial accounts provide a historic record of the monies which have come into and gone out of an organization. Management accounts monitor income and expenditure against budgets and targets, and provide a basis for forecasting future performance.

CASE STUDY

Training and Enterprise Councils (TECs) exist to encourage the development of both businesses and individuals in local areas. They are funded mainly through money from the Department of Education and Employment (DfEE).

Each year, TECs develop business plans, which are submitted to the Government for approval and funding. This funding depends on the achievement of targets. Failure to achieve these targets not only threatens the financial viability of a TEC, but also leads to a risk that its licence will not be renewed for the following year.

Predictably, the DfEE demands that money given to a TEC should be very carefully managed. In fact, in 1997, one TEC in the West Midlands was closed down as a result of poor financial control.

It is clear from this that the survival of a TEC is dependent on its ability both to make a persuasive case for funding and to control its finances to the satisfaction of the Government.

MARKETING

The Chartered Institute of Marketing defines the marketing function as:

---

the management process responsible for defining, antici-
pating and satisfying customer needs profitably.

This process can, in turn, be broken down into a range of activities:

- Market research finds out what customers want, what they are currently buying and how much they are pre-pared to pay.
- Advertising and sales promotion are ways of informing customers and persuading them to try a product or service.
- Sales management may involve telephone sales staff or a field sales force.
- Distribution is to do with getting the product or service physically to the customer.
- Product management involves developing, improving and updating in line with changes to customer needs and competitor activity.

Historically, the marketing function has been applied to external customers – those outside the business who paid with their own money for the goods and services which the business produced. The customers may have been members of the general public in the case of retail outlets, other businesses in the case of heavy engineering, or taxpayers in the case of local government, schools or hospitals. Even charities have customers. Somewhat cynically, it has been argued that a charity's customers pay for the benefit of being relieved of guilt when confronted with others less fortunate than themselves. Or, slightly less cynically, for the 'feel-good' factor of knowing they are helping others.

Regardless of the activities in which they are engaged, all organizations need to communicate with customers, offer customers something which they will see as being of benefit to them and persuade them that the benefit is worth paying for.

The annual 'Children in Need' appeal is designed to persuade people to part with their money in order to support a wide range of children's charities. Those who contribute receive no obvious benefit. Or do they?

- Many of the fund-raising activities are carried out by groups of friends, neighbours or work colleagues – a social benefit.
- A high proportion of the money raised goes directly to the charities – a 'feel-good' benefit.
- The appeal receives extensive media coverage – people are attracted by the chance of appearing on television or in the newspapers.
- It is also the subject of a night-long BBC programme – people are prepared to pay (indirectly) for the benefit of an evening's entertainment.
- Monies raised are compared with those of previous years – an appeal to the competitive spirit.

As the marketing manager in our debate pointed out, it is the marketing function which ensures that an organization continues to attract the funding it needs by keeping its offerings in line with customer needs and wants.

However, as Chapter 4 of this book will point out, current management thinking has extended the definition of 'customer' to include colleagues within the organization. As a result, every activity in an organization is being encouraged to measure its success in marketing terms:

- Are we giving our customers what they want?
- Is our service efficient enough to meet their needs?
- How well do we compete with alternative suppliers? (For example, if we make components, are they as reliable or as cheap as those from an outside supplier?)

Looked at from this point of view, marketing ceases to be a specialist responsibility with a focus on external customers. Instead, it becomes the responsibility of every member of staff throughout the organization, based on the uncomfortable recognition that there is no such thing as a captive customer. Assuming that the organization is willing to allow it, any activity, from warehousing to payroll preparation to training to transport to selling, could potentially be carried out by an agent or contractor.

PERSONNEL

Increasingly, organizations are abandoning the 'personnel' title in favour of the grander term 'human resources'. There is little justification for this change as far as the meanings are concerned. Rather, it indicates a change in status of the function.

Traditionally, personnel has been regarded largely as a branch of administration – there to hire staff, pay them, train them, draw up employment contracts and, when necessary, to make sure redundancies are legal. Only very rarely has personnel had any involvement with the strategic direction of an organization.

The move to the 'human resources' title reflects this strategic involvement. In growing numbers of organizations, strategic decisions are now being taken, not only on the basis of:

- Can we afford it?
- Do customers want it?
- Have we got the technology?

But also on the basis of:

- Have we enough people?
- Do they have the right skills?
- Where will tomorrow's managers come from?

These are all human resources questions and go to the heart of an organization's ability to survive and prosper. But, of course, people are no more important as a resource than money or customers.

OPERATIONS

So is our production supervisor right to argue that operations is the most important function?

The answer to that question depends largely on how we define the term. If we view operations as synonymous with manufacturing or service delivery, then it is as important as finance, marketing and personnel; but no more so. From that viewpoint, it is one of four functions, all of which depend on each other.

On the other hand, we have already had several clues which suggest that operations management means more than just manufacturing or service delivery. In the Introduction to this book, we defined operations as:

> the activities carried out by an organization to provide the service to customers or clients which is its basic reason for existing.

There are other definitions which make similar points:

> Virtually everyone with a management responsibility is involved in managing operations – because almost every management job requires the efficient use of resources to achieve the defined outcomes, which in most cases relate to the needs of customers.
> (Professor Ray Wild, Henley Management College)

> Managing the physical resources necessary to create products in sufficient quantities to meet market requirements.
> (J. Mapes and C. C. New, *The Gower Handbook of Management*, Gower Publishing, 1987)

The emphasis on customer needs is also a reminder that customers can be internal as well as external. Add to that the idea from the Introduction to this book that operations management involves adding value through the transformation of inputs into outputs and we are suddenly faced with a rather daunting prospect: that all managers in every function in every organization are responsible for managing operations. If that is the case, then operations must be the most important of our four functions because it is central to all of them. The remainder of this chapter explains how operations management works in a wide range of industries and activities.

Operations management in manufacturing

The production supervisor in our original debate made most of the points which are relevant to this heading. In broad terms, the manufacturing process takes inputs in the form of raw materials, components or subassemblies and adds value by transforming them into finished goods. Of course, the process is more complicated than that brief description suggests. Operations management in manufacturing must ensure that the necessary inputs are available in the right quantities and at the right times; that machines are set up to the correct specifications; that machine operators are available; that outputs meet quality standards and are delivered in a way that meets the needs of the next internal customer in line – packing, perhaps, or warehousing or transport.

Operations management in retailing

In manufacturing, it is easy to see the change in form or content which the transformation process brings about. In retailing, the transformation is less obvious, but it is still there. Take a petrol station, for example. Its primary products – petrol and oil – come out of the ground in huge quantities many hundreds or thousands of miles away from where the final customer – the motorist – wants them. The petrol station adds value by making them available at convenient locations. It brings about a transformation in both form and location. Or take another example – that of a DIY supermarket. The inputs here are the products on the shelves, but also the expertise of the staff. The customer brings a need – to build a wall, perhaps. A member of staff offers advice on the products to buy, explains how to do the job or provides an explanatory leaflet. The transformation here is that of the customer – from someone with neither the resources nor the knowledge to build a wall, to someone with both.

Operations management in a service industry

In Western Europe more than half of the workforce is employed in the service sector. In the USA three out of four jobs are in the service sector. In most cases, the primary input is the expertise of the worker. These are the jobs that Peter Drucker describes as the 'knowledge workers'. It is tempting to think of jobs in the service sector as involving complex and rather obscure skills – computer programming, for example, or management consultancy, or transport planning. But similar transformations take place as a result of less sophisticated work. Picture the service department of your local garage. You take your car into the garage because it keeps stalling at traffic lights. The mechanic uses his or her expertise and the test equipment available to confirm that petrol is getting to the engine. So it's not a fuel problem. Using his or her experience, the mechanic then asks you when it happens – all the time, or only when the engine has warmed up? The latter, you say. So he or she takes the car out to warm it up and notices the temperature gauge never reaches full temperature. This suggests that the thermostat may be faulty. The mechanic removes it, checks it and confirms that it is not working properly. He or she then fits a replacement and the problem is solved.

- ■ What have the inputs and outputs been in this process?
- ■ What sort of transformation has taken place?
- ■ What value has the process added?

Now compare your thoughts with Figure 1.1.

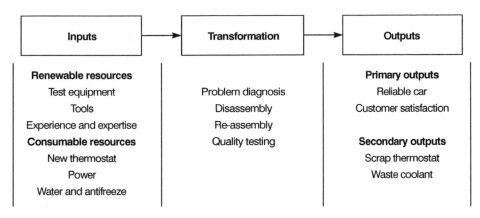

Inputs	Transformation	Outputs
Renewable resources		**Primary outputs**
Test equipment	Problem diagnosis	Reliable car
Tools	Disassembly	Customer satisfaction
Experience and expertise	Re-assembly	
Consumable resources	Quality testing	**Secondary outputs**
New thermostat		Scrap thermostat
Power		Waste coolant
Water and antifreeze		

Figure 1.1

Operations management in a charity

Charities in the UK operate in a bewildering variety of ways. You may think of charity shops selling new and second-hand goods, street collections, volunteer services such as the Samaritans or hospital visiting, animal sanctuaries or the Royal National Lifeboat Institute. All or any of these offer practical day-to-day examples of operations management.

Take charity shops as an obvious example. Operations management involves transforming public goodwill into saleable goods, volunteer goodwill into trained staff, donations and revenue into the services the charity is designed to support and into the running expenses of the shop. Street collections involve mobilizing teams of volunteer collectors, providing collecting boxes, arranging the safe transport of the money, counting and distributing it.

The operation of a volunteer service like the Samaritans involves recruiting, training and scheduling volunteers, making available telephones, furniture and accommodation and publicizing the service. An animal sanctuary requires accommodation. It also requires volunteers, vets, transport and drivers. A major operational task for the RNLI is the design and commissioning of boats to meet the needs of both the volunteer crews and those whom the boats are designed to rescue.

Operations management in a hospital

You will have recognized by now that operations management can be considered at two levels: first, at the big-picture level, as the transformation of inputs to achieve the satisfaction of the final customer; and, second, at the detailed level, where it involves consideration of individual processes and activities from the viewpoint of the next customer in the chain.

As you would expect, this distinction applies equally to a hospital. The big picture involves the transformation of sick patients into well people through the inputs of medical expertise, drugs, surgical equipment, catering and accommodation. At the detailed level, we could consider any of a thousand separate processes. For example, consider the preparation of a patient for an operation. In this case, the next customer in the chain is the surgeon. The surgeon needs the patient to be sedated, the operating site to be cleaned and the patient delivered to the operating theatre. These are, in turn, the responsibilities of the ward staff and of the porters. At this detailed, or micro, level the transformation is one of form and location – from a conscious patient in the ward to a sedated patient in the theatre.

Operations management in a school

As you would expect, the two levels of operations management apply here as well. At the big-picture, or macro, level we can regard the transformation in a school as being from uneducated to educated pupils, or from pupils without skills or qualifications to pupils with these. Value is added to the benefit of the individual pupil, employers or universities and society as a whole.

Once again, there are hundreds of examples of micro-level transformations. The catering staff, for example, who may be in the employ of the school or of a specialist subcontractor meet the needs of pupils, parents and teachers by transforming raw materials (food) into cooked meals. They change the form of the raw materials, and the content, by adding spices and seasoning to provide added value in the form of nutrition and stamina at an economic price. At least, that's the way the process ought to work! Not always, of course. Complaints about the price and quality of school meals are simply an indication that, in some cases, operations managers have not given enough thought to the needs of their customers.

Operations management in a government department

Our earlier definition of operations as:

the activities carried out by an organization to provide the service to customers or clients which is its basic reason for existing.

presents a fundamental challenge to a government department. This is not because the definition does not apply, but because a government department is heavily influenced by both the demands of the party in power and by the expectations of the electorate. As a result, government departments often find that their customers come to challenge what has been seen historically as their 'basic reason for existence' and, by extension, the service they provide.

CASE STUDY

It would seem reasonable to argue that the Ministry of Defence (MoD) exists to defend the people and territory of the United Kingdom. However, the reality is less simple.

The MoD is the largest government department, with over 100 000 staff. It absorbs an annual budget of many billions of pounds of taxpayers' money.

In times of war and of obvious international threat, such as during the Cold War, there have been few questions about the role and importance of the MoD. Now the issues are less obvious.

Customers – in the shape of the Government and the electorate – are asking questions such as:

- Do we have any real enemies?
- If so, who are they?
- Can we justify the cost of MoD civilian staff and the armed forces?
- Could some of the MoD budget be better spent elsewhere?

These and similar questions have resulted in serious doubt amongst both customers and MoD staff about the value added by the Ministry. At a macro level, there is confusion about its basic reason for existence.

However, at a micro level, there are still purchase orders to raise, bills to pay, staff to train, vacancies to fill and stores to buy.

In Chapter 2 of this book, we return to the theme of how operations management contributes to the achievement of strategic objectives. As far as government departments are concerned, it is important to recognize two major issues: firstly, that operations at macro level – which depend for their success on the understanding and commitment of staff at all levels – are seriously hampered if people do not know how the work they do contributes to the big picture; and, secondly, that the fundamental question 'Why do we exist?' is being asked, not only in the Ministry of Defence, but also in the National Health Service, Social Security, the Department of Transport and elsewhere.

Operations management in local government

Operations managers in local government have the benefit of being much closer to their final customers than do their counterparts in national government. But is that really true?

Who do you see as the customer of local government? Locally, it is reasonable to define customers as shopkeepers, rate-payers, road-users, school-children, parents and, in general, the local electorate. But, at the same time, local government is accountable to political parties, both at a local and national level, and limited by national government as to the amount of tax it can collect and, in consequence, the resources it can allocate.

As a result, at a macro level, local government has several groups of customers to satisfy, whose needs may well be contradictory. And yet, at the micro level, there will always be the next customer in the chain with an urgent need for authorization to redecorate a council house, the resources to repair a damaged street light, the money to recruit a new teacher or to buy textbooks.

Consequently, operations managers in local government are faced with the same problems as those facing operations managers everywhere:

- Who are my priority customers?
- How do I use my resources to achieve maximum output?
- How can I streamline or improve activities to achieve outputs more efficiently?

We will return to these questions again in Chapters 3 and 4 of this book.

Project, batch and continuous operations

So far in this chapter, we have emphasized that the essential process of operations management is the transformation of inputs or resources into something which is of value to the customer. We have also pointed out that such a definition of operations management applies at both a macro and a micro level. To finish the chapter, we will look briefly at three different types of operations, raising in the process some of the systems and resource management issues which we will examine in greater detail later in this book.

The descriptions we shall be using

- project operations
- batch operations
- continuous operations

have their origin in the vocabulary of manufacturing. However, as we have seen, there are fundamental similarities between operations management across a wide range of industries and activities. So it should come as no surprise that these descriptions are as relevant to service, government, health care or education as they are to manufacturing. The distinction between these three operating modes stems from the relative continuity of each system.

Project operations

Sometimes known as 'job operations', these provide products on a 'one-off' basis. Each output is unique and prepared to meet the specific needs of an individual customer. Here are some examples:

- the market-testing of a new product
- the analysis of the performance of a potential acquisition target
- the design and manufacture of a new battleship
- a decorator asked to repaint a single home
- a hole-in-the-heart operation
- the introduction of a one-way traffic system.

Discontinuity is the principal characteristic of a project operation. It works by bringing together a series of well-tried processes (micro operations) but in a way which is customized to the requirement of a specific customer.

The main difficulty with project operations comes from the need to set up and resource each such operation from scratch. Any organization involved in project operations either needs to keep expert staff and specialist equipment lying idle until called upon – with all the cost implications that involves – or else trust that it can find subcontractors to carry out parts of the project, raising doubts about quality and availability if it does so.

Batch operations

The distinguishing feature of batch operations is that the same resources (people and equipment) are used to provide a range of goods or services. The following are examples of batch operations:

- a biscuit manufacturer using the same machines and operators to produce, for example, custard creams or bourbons according to demand
- a local authority renovating a group of similar houses in the same neighbourhood at the same time
- a school processing a 'batch' of pupils through the syllabus of a single examination

- a car manufacturer producing and promoting a range of 'special editions'
- a doctor's surgery offering antenatal classes at a specific time each week.

The output pattern of batch operations is discontinuous but regular or repetitive. Such operations involve significant set-up costs but bring benefits over project operations in the shape of economies of scale. Nevertheless, they also bring drawbacks in terms of customer satisfaction because of the waiting time involved. That is why, in a manufacturing context, batch operations are often used to make-for-stock.

Continuous operations

Known alternatively as 'line operations', the dominant feature here is that of continuity, with a high degree of repetition in work patterns. Line operations depend on sophisticated production equipment, which in turn demands significant capital investment. As a consequence, three-shift, seven-days-a-week working is commonplace in line operations. The most obvious examples come from manufacturing: car production lines, or the extrusion of plastic pipe. But there are others:

- natural gas extraction
- twenty-four-hour shop opening
- emergency services (police, fire, ambulance).

Continuous operations bring significant cost advantages because of reduced downtime and set-up time. Nevertheless, they are becoming increasingly inconsistent with customer demand. Henry Ford's well-known dictum that 'You can have any colour so long as it's black' is axiomatic of the impact of continuous operations on customer choice.

What sort of operation are you responsible for – project, batch or continuous? Which is the best? As we shall see in later chapters, operational design walks a narrow line between efficiency and cost-effectiveness on one side and customer satisfaction on the other. As we have seen, the move from project to batch to continuous operations increases efficiency and cost-effectiveness while reducing consistency with customer requirements and expectations – except, of course, that the same progression reduces the cost of the product or service, which in turn lowers the price, which in turn increases customer satisfaction. The impact is the same whether customers are internal or external. So is it possible to identify one best form of operational design out of the three we have described?

As previously explained, project operations offer an exact match with customer requirements, but at a high price. They are suited to customers who recognize the uniqueness of their need, but are likely to be unpopular with those who believe that they could have done just as well – but more cheaply – by buying 'off the shelf'.

At the other extreme, continuous operations result in products or services which are identical to thousands or millions of others. If you are looking for a new gas cooker, you probably will not mind that there are several identical models in the same street. But you will be less pleased to turn up at a party to find that three other guests are wearing the same dress as you!

As customers have come increasingly to demand products and services which meet their individual needs, so suppliers have adapted continuous operations so that they can offer the benefits of batch, or even project, operation.

CASE STUDY

Marks and Spencer (M&S) offers clothes in a wide range of sizes. However, there is always the occasional customer who needs a size outside the norm.

In the past, the answer would have been: 'I'm sorry, you'll have to look elsewhere.' Now, though, it's different.

The company has now negotiated with its suppliers that, on request, any garment can be made in any size. Because of the value of their M&S contracts, suppliers are prepared to produce 'one-off' items in line with customer requirements.

There are other examples. Aided by new paint technology, Land Rover are willing to match any colour a customer asks for on a new Range Rover. Even service companies are going down the same route. In the past, if your television gave trouble, you would be told the day when the engineer would arrive, but not anymore. Now, you can expect to be told the hour as well.

It would be dangerous to draw any long-term conclusions from these examples. All we can say is that, at the time of writing, suppliers seem to be placing customer satisfaction ahead of efficiency and cost-effectiveness in their list of priorities. Whether this is the result of an increased focus on customers, or of fear of the competition, is difficult to say. For the time being, though, the priority for operations management is customer satisfaction.

COMPETENCE SELF-ASSESSMENT

1   Consider your own organization. Which does it see as most important: finance, marketing, personnel or operations?
2   Do you agree with that assessment? If not, what could you do to change it in your own area of responsibility?
3   Who are your organization's final customers?
4   How well does it meet their requirements and expectations?
5   What improvements would you recommend?
6   Who are your next customers in the chain?
7   How well do you meet their requirements and expectations?
8   What improvements could you make?
9   How efficient, cost-effective and customer satisfying is the operational mode (project, batch, continuous) for which you are responsible?
10   What changes would you make, and why?

2 The organizational context

Increasingly, the trend in organizational design today is towards smaller, more autonomous business units. Evidence for this trend takes several forms:

- replacement of traditional hierarchies, with all decisions taken at the centre, by decentralization of decision-making
- the incorporation of support services (like finance and personnel) into the activities of business units
- the fragmentation of multiple product-lines into single-product activities, either for manufacture, marketing, or both.

The arguments for this approach (which is commonly called decentralization or federalism) are that:

- hierarchical organizations are ponderous and slow to react. As we shall see later in this chapter, speed of response to change is now critical to organizational survival and success.
- centralized control reduces motivation and innovation. Employee expectations have changed from a comparative

willingness to follow orders and instructions to the expectation that they will be consulted and involved in decisions.
- multilevel organizations are excessively costly. Questions are now being regularly asked about the costs and benefits of layers of management and the contribution of support functions.
- decisions taken at the centre are divorced from both customers and staff. Put more strongly, this argument is simply that decisions taken at the centre are divorced from reality!

Symptoms of this move from centralized to decentralized decision-making are:

- a heavy emphasis on 'empowerment' of all staff in the organization. We shall return to this theme in Chapter 10 of this book.
- extensive 'delayering', by removing layers of management and pushing the responsibility for decision-making lower down the organization.
- the recognition of colleagues and other functions in the organization as 'internal customers'. This approach makes everyone in the organization responsible for identifying and satisfying customer needs.
- the delegation of budgets and operational control to far more junior staff than was traditionally the case.

CASE STUDY

In Mazda – and this is typical of most Japanese car manufacturers – all production workers are entitled to stop the line if they consider that production quality is not satisfactory. It is then the responsibility of the workers – operating as a Total Quality team – to identify and resolve the problem.

The picture which emerges from all this is of small groups of contented staff happily managing their own working lives without the need for centralized guidance or direction. And if you think that sounds too good to be true, you would be right!

QUESTION

■ What risks can you see in a move to decentralized decision-making?
■ What else needs to happen to make sure it is effective?

THE RISKS OF DECENTRALIZATION

The trend we have described appears to offer several benefits – to staff, customers and the organization alike. Indeed, it is a central theme of many of the 'excellence' texts published in the 1980s. For example:

> On the other hand, we have the excellent companies. They are big. They have enviable records of growth, innovation and consequent wealth. Clearly, the odds are stacked against them. Yet they do it just the same. Perhaps the most important element of their enviable track record is an ability to be big and yet to act small at the same time. A concomitant essential apparently is that they encourage the entrepreneurial spirit among their people, because they push autonomy remarkably far down the line ...
> (T. J. Peters and R. H. Waterman, *In Search of Excellence*, Harper and Row, 1982)

> We have not so far been able to find an example of a highly successful British manufacturing company with a heavily centralized organization.
> (W. Goldsmith and D. Clutterbuck, *The Winning Streak*, Penguin, 1984)

But it would be a mistake to assume that the move from centralized control to autonomous operation is risk-free.

Experience shows that the risks fall into four categories:

■ expectations
■ expertise
■ control
■ co-ordination.

Expectations

Under this heading, we need to consider both staff and customer expectations. For most organizations, decentralization and increased autonomy are initiatives which postdate the arrival of staff members by many years. Recruited into an organization where decisions were taken by senior management and the employees' job was to do as they were told, staff can often find that they are suddenly expected to take far more personal responsibility than was the norm when they joined.

CASE STUDY

The British factory of Continental Tyres was threatened with closure when it proved unable to match the quality and productivity of its European counterparts. The senior management mounted a factory-wide initiative to seek suggestions for improvement from staff at all levels. Whilst the initiative was generally welcomed, significant numbers of staff complained that they were being asked to do the thinking that management was paid to do.

Increased delegation may also not meet customer expectations. Customers who have come to expect attention from a senior manager often feel slighted if they are now to be attended by someone more junior.

CASE STUDY

In Marks and Spencer's Oxford Street store, junior managers used to take it in turns to pretend to be the Branch Manager, in order that customers with a complaint could speak to someone they considered to have the authority to deal with it.

Expertise

We have pointed out that increased operating autonomy often goes with the removal of layers of management. Whilst bringing cost benefits, this approach may also involve the loss of valuable expertise and experience.

> **CASE STUDY**
>
> In order to cut costs, one of the UK's high street banks offered early retirement to a large group of long-standing Head Office managers. However, it then found that no one was left who had the experience to take the decisions for which they had been responsible. As a result, the bank was forced to hire back some of its retired managers on consultancy contracts.

In addition, the removal of central support functions may require remaining managers to take on specialist responsibilities – for example, the implementation of contract terms – for which they lack the expertise.

Control

We have already mentioned the argument in favour of decentralization: that centralized control reduces motivation and innovation. This does not change the fact that operational control remains an essential activity. Delegated or decentralized control brings the risk that different parts of the business will operate different or inconsistent standards, thereby leading to our fourth risk.

Co-ordination

Poor co-ordination between operating units leads to two distinct problems. The first can sometimes be turned into an advantage. The second never can.

The first problem relates to the perception of the organization by the customer. If different parts of the organization offer different standards, prices and quality, whilst attempting to promote itself as a consistent whole, its image will suffer and it will be extremely difficult to formulate and promote a marketing message which can reconcile the inconsistencies.

Some organizations, however, take advantage of such inconsistencies by positioning different brands at different price or quality points in the market. The motor trade offers several excellent examples of this.

> **CASE STUDY**
>
> When Toyota made the strategic decision to enter the luxury car market, it established through market research that the Toyota name was too closely identified with smaller family cars to be carried by a luxury model. It therefore

developed the Lexus brand, which is applied exclusively to its top-of-the-range cars.

Jaguar is owned by Ford. However, the brand is sold through different outlets and, until the recent decision to build the X400 baby Jaguar at Ford's Halewood plant, was produced at different factories. Even the X400 production line at Halewood is to operate to different quality standards, and to be staffed by different and specially trained production workers from the Ford lines.

Volkswagen (VW) took advantage of the opportunity to invest in Eastern Europe by buying Skoda. Although new Skoda models have benefited from Volkswagen design and common components, VW has deliberately positioned Skoda at a different price point, thus giving access to two separate markets.

■ The second co-ordination problem, however, is inherently obvious from the three examples we have quoted. In each case, the decision to offer different brands with different characteristics resulted from a strategic plan formulated and co-ordinated at the highest level of the company. So, for example, the price and quality differences between Toyota and Lexus didn't just happen – they were deliberately planned and implemented. It is clear that there is a limit beyond which decision-making and autonomy cannot be delegated, if the organization is to implement a coherent strategy. Or, to put it more simply: someone at the top needs to take the big decisions

What counts as 'the big decisions' appears to vary from sector to sector. As an example of this, it is worth returning to Goldsmith and Clutterbuck's *The Winning Streak* for a moment. Our earlier quote from this book is part of a longer section. Here it is in full:

In our sample of companies we have, with minor exceptions, two camps. At the one extreme are the decentralists, who operate as federations of independent small units. At the other end are the centralists, who have large functional departments at headquarters and very limited autonomy at operating level. With one exception,

> the centralists are all retailers; we have so far not been able to find an example of a highly successful British manufacturing company with a heavily centralized organization.

This centralized decision-making in multisite retailing is designed to achieve consistency in design, image, presentation, stock and pricing. As a ridiculous example, just picture the customer confusion and irritation if Boots had a blue fascia in one town but red in another, sold toothpaste in one store but not in another and charged different prices for the same item in different branches!

Of course, the same does not apply to manufacturing. Here, it is reasonable for operations managers in different locations to make their own decisions about the external sourcing of components – which suppliers to use and the price and delivery details of the contract – and even about the wages to pay, if one factory is in a high-cost area with low unemployment and another in a low-cost area with high unemployment. Nevertheless, the need for co-ordination still applies. If different factories are producing the same product, mechanisms need to exist to ensure that the product does the same job and meets the same standards, regardless of where it comes from.

CASE STUDY

Jacob's Biscuits used to manufacture the same product at factories in both England and Southern Ireland. The Irish biscuits were both cheaper and of higher quality. The company tried, but failed, to achieve consistency between the two products. Total production for that line was then concentrated in Southern Ireland.

In most cases, operational co-ordination in charities is limited. Dependent largely on volunteers, charities are willing to sacrifice consistency in favour of delegated decision-making. Nevertheless, there are exceptions. A few years ago, Oxfam made a significant financial investment to achieve consistency in the image and decor of its high street outlets. This was not a painless exercise. Many supporters objected that the money spent on upgrading the shops should have been allocated directly to the Third World causes which Oxfam exists to help.

Government departments are a totally different matter. It would be wholly unacceptable, for example, if income tax or VAT were calculated in different ways in different parts of the country. The Civil Service approach to ensuring consistency in such activities is to publish detailed procedure or operations manuals, which specify exactly what processes to follow and how calculations should be made. Nevertheless, even in the Civil Service there is a growing trend towards delegated decision-making.

In the past, little attempt was made to co-ordinate the activities of individual schools and hospitals. However, things have changed. The introduction of performance league tables for schools and of freedom for GPs to choose where to send patients for hospital treatment is intended to achieve greater consistency of performance by bringing the performance of the worst up to the standard of the best.

EFFECTIVE DECENTRALIZATION

The keys to effective decentralization are remedies to the risks we have already described. In order to address the issue of staff and customer expectations, the following are important:

- Ensure that staff recognize the nature and responsibilities of their jobs. For new staff, this is relatively straightforward. It involves preparing job descriptions which are accurate and realistic, evaluating each job and ensuring that wage or salary levels are competitive with those on the wider job market.

    For existing staff, the process is more demanding. It may require jobs to be redefined, regraded and pay adjusted. It is not adequate simply to assume that staff will be satisfied purely with the challenge of greater responsibility.

- Recognize and address the need for training. Countless 'empowerment' initiatives have failed as a result of crediting staff with the instinctive ability to make decisions and implement improvements, after years during which such instincts have been treated as a disciplinary offence.

- Implement a change in management style. The traditional 'command and control' style expects obedience without question and penalizes mistakes. By contrast, delegated decision-making involves a willingness for judgements to be questioned, and mistakes to be made, in pursuit of improvement and innovation. Clifford and Cavanagh (*The Winning Performance*, Sidgwick and Jackson, 1985) quote the following example:

At MCI, the 'other' long-distance telephone company, making and learning from mistakes seems to be a central part of the management catechism. We interviewed twenty-five senior managers at MCI to discern the critical elements of its corporate culture. The first conversation was with Bill McGowan, the chief executive, who, after answering our questions, concluded the interview by saying: 'Don't forget, we make a lot of mistakes around this place. Have from the beginning. But so long as somebody doesn't keep making the same mistake over and over again, we can live with it and recover ...'. What distinguishes the way these winning companies manage mistakes is that they make them on a small scale, encourage lots of experiments and dedicate their energy to fixing them rather than attributing fault.

- Communicate with customers. As with any marketing initiative, moving customer responsibility further down the organization needs customers to understand the benefits. They'll have easier and quicker access. The individual concerned will understand their needs better. Actions and decisions will be taken more quickly.

  Delegating customer contact may be a cost saving or an efficiency measure. It may be because the person who used to have that responsibility has been made redundant – the job has disappeared. But that is all bad news which should remain internal. If you're going to sell the change, find the good news which benefits the customer.

The matter of expertise can be resolved primarily by not getting carried away by management theory! Delayering and delegated decision-making are not automatic sources of performance improvement. Rather, their effectiveness depends on a careful analysis of:

- the operational processes and control systems in place
- the nature and culture of the business
- the quality and experience of the staff.

So, for example, in a manufacturing business where production processes are simple, effective systems exist to monitor quality and output, and junior staff are familiar with the processes, the removal of layers of management is likely to be successful.

CASE STUDY

LMG Packaging produces printed paper and plastic packaging for a range of industries, including food and medical supplies. In order to upgrade its production technology, the company bought new, computer-controlled machines from Italy. The machines incorporated a range of devices to monitor production tolerances, the outputs from which appear on screens attached to the machines. The company trained its machine operators to interpret the displays and make adjustments based upon them – a task which had previously been done by team leaders on the old manually controlled machines. They were thus able not only to enlarge the machine operators' jobs, but also to restructure the teams, reducing the number of team leaders through transfer and natural wastage.

On the other hand, in a sophisticated business with complex processes, where control is exercised by experienced supervisors but junior staff are not very capable, the cost of introducing new control systems and, quite possibly, recruiting a new cohort of junior staff, may well make it preferable to stick with multiple levels of management, regardless of what the textbooks say!

We have already introduced the subject of control. Effective control starts by finding answers to the following questions:

- What are the critical success factors in the business, or in the part of the business for which I am responsible?
- What do my customers expect from me?
- How can those success factors and customer expectations be translated into measurable objectives?
- What monitoring systems will be necessary to measure performance against objectives?
- What performance tolerances will be acceptable?

Quantitative objectives are relatively easy to set and measure: machine output, gross and net profit, calls made or business won per salesperson, for example. Qualitative objectives are less easy. How do you measure:

- the relevance and effectiveness of training?
- customer satisfaction?
- staff motivation?

Stop for a moment to see if you can think of operational controls which would measure those three factors, then compare your answers with ours:

■ Relevance and effectiveness of training. Most training operations use some kind of 'happy sheet' at the end of a training event. Typically, these ask delegates whether the event was relevant to their needs using a scale like that in Figure 2.1, which can be translated into numbers.

5	4	3	2	1
Very	Fairly	To some extent	Not very	Not at all

Figure 2.1

The effectiveness of training cannot be assessed at the event itself. The measurement of the factor requires a monitoring process which asks managers to assess the trainee's performance before and after the event. Provided that the manager is given descriptions of performance at different standards ('mastery', 'excellence', 'competence', 'needs improvement', 'needs considerable improvement', for example) it is again possible to quantify the results.

■ Customer satisfaction. A number of indirect measures can be applied to this factor. For example:
■ numbers of complaints
■ volume of repeat business
■ regular customer satisfaction surveys.

■ Staff motivation. This factor can be measured indirectly by recording:
■ staff turnover
■ length of service
■ numbers of grievances
■ absentee levels
■ days lost due to industrial action.

Success factors, customer expectations, measurable objectives and monitoring systems are all important issues. However, the internal customer makes customer expectations the most critical.

Which brings us to the issue of co-ordination. As we shall see in more detail in Chapter 4 of this book, operations management adds value to the final customer by spanning a range of functions, as the manufacturing diagram in Figure 2.2 makes clear.

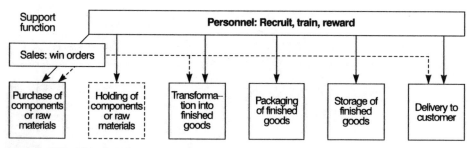

Figure 2.2   The manufacturing process

As we explained in Chapter 1, the sales or marketing function promotes the product, builds customer desire for it, sells it and takes the order. This in turn results in manufacturing activity. However, the factory is also dependent on the components or raw materials bought by the purchasing function. Finished goods are then packaged, held in the warehouse, then delivered to the customer.

The need for co-ordination throughout this process is obvious:

- The factory needs to know from sales how much of each product to make.
- Purchasing needs to know the factory's production schedule, in order to buy the right quantities of components or raw materials to make them available at the right time.
- The warehouse needs to know what to deliver, when and to whom.

As we mentioned earlier, operations management takes place at both a macro and a micro level. Chapter 3 describes the micro operations which are necessary to ensure the continuous availability of the right resources.

We shall now consider the involvement of operations management in 'the big picture' planning – the development of strategy.

STRATEGY, MISSION AND GOALS

Theodore Levitt, the well-known American management guru, once said: 'If you don't know where you're going, any road will take you there.' This seems obvious. It implies that, unless an organization is clear, at least in general terms, about what it exists to do, the customers it intends to serve, the products and services it will offer and how big it wants to be, it will be impossible to take meaningful decisions and actions related to:

- resources
- budgets
- product and service quality
- staffing levels
- staff quantity, training, expertise and reward.

It is therefore surprising that research continues to show that a high proportion of organizations – particularly in the small and medium-sized categories – continue to operate on a 'hunch and gut feel' basis.

Equally surprising is the fact that so many operations do indeed follow a strategic planning process, but fail to achieve their goals. A recent survey found that 70 per cent of businesses had failed to achieve their merger and acquisition objectives and 79 per cent had failed to implement the customer service initiatives contained in their plan.

So how *should* the strategic planning process work? Francis J. Kelly and Heather Mayfield Kelly, in their book *What They Really Teach You at the Harvard Business School* (Piatkus, 1987), describe the Harvard approach as follows:

> The first step in developing a strong business-policy analysis is to identify and analyse the 'immovable object' elements in the environment in which a decision is being made – the elements over which one has no control. These are called *fixed elements*. These elements, which cannot be manipulated by management, form the constraints within which management must operate ... First, the competitive environment must be assessed. Companies must determine what business they are in and who the main competitors are ... after analysing the competition, carefully assess your own company's resources. What are the company's major strengths in relation to its competitors – product quality? Lower cost? Marketing

clout? Greater financial resources? What are its major weaknesses – product quality? Distribution? Sales force? The best corporate strategies are those that draw upon a company's strengths while minimizing its weaknesses.

Third, society's expectations for the enterprise must be analysed. Does society expect the firm to reap huge profits? Pay a lot in taxes? Provide jobs? Invest locally? What will anger society? How important is public opinion, especially bad public opinion? Will it affect company performance? . . .

Management values is another important area that needs analysis. In what direction will the values of its management lead a company? What directions will they prohibit? Does management most value growth and profits or is a stable liveable work environment more important? Is performance most valued or honesty and loyalty to the company? . . .

Given the constraints placed on a company and outlined in the fixed elements analysis, management must then work with the many variables over which it does have control to construct its business policy. These controllable elements must be analysed in order to create the best possible corporate strategy for a particular company, given its unique position in the marketplace.

Marketing policies must be analysed. What should the company produce? How should these products be positioned? How should they be priced? What is the best way to distribute those products? How should the product be advertised and promoted?

Manufacturing policies need careful attention. What type of manufacturing process is best to produce the type and quantity of products the company desires? Where should manufacturing and distribution facilities be located? Should the company manufacture continually or seasonally? What role will new technologies play in operations?

Integrated financial policies must be developed. What performance goals does the company want to set in terms of profits, operating margins, and return on capital? Will the company's funds come from operations, debt or equity? How much ownership will management retain? How much will employees own? How much will the public own?

Research and development policies must also be set. What percentage of sales will be ploughed back into

R&D? Will R&D effort be long-term in nature or more short-term/application-oriented? Will R&D be done for the whole company at the corporate level or will it be done within each division? Who will manage R&D operations? Are R&D joint ventures in the firm's best interest?

Human resources policies are also critical. What type of people will the company seek to employ? How will employees be compensated? Will salaries be high or low? Will compensation be all salary or less salary and greater opportunities for bonuses? Issues of corporate structure must be investigated. How will the company be structured to maximize success in the marketplace?

The diagram resulting from these two stages of analysis (fixed element analysis, controllable element analysis) is shown in Figure 2.3.

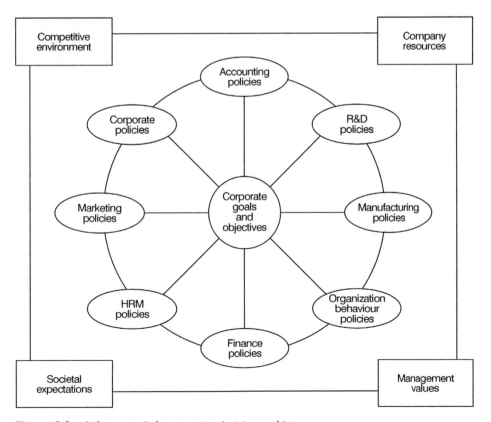

Figure 2.3   A framework for strategic decision-making

This model – and the questions and issues raised by the Harvard process – are broadly consistent with other strategic planning models. And, although there are references throughout to manufacturing and trading companies, you should have no difficulty in recognizing those which are relevant to your organization, whatever its reason for existence may be.

Operations management and strategic planning

You may be wondering what the strategic planning process has to do with you. There are two answers to this, each of which is inherent in points already made in this book.

Top-down and bottom-up planning

In a traditional hierarchy, strategic decisions were taken by top management and passed down through the organization for implementation. This is the old 'command and control' culture previously mentioned.

Nowadays, though, organizations are recognizing that all strategic decisions have operational consequences, at both a macro and a micro level. And, at the micro level, it is the staff closest to the action who are likely to be best placed to decide what is possible and what should be done.

It is not suggested that strategic plans should be simply an accumulation of micro-level operational plans. The lack of co-ordination and cross-functional consistency which would result from such an approach would be devastating: all the bits of an organization would be pulling in different directions.

Instead, the modern response to strategic planning is to combine a top-down with a bottom-up approach. In other words, senior management fixes the mission of the organization – a short, clear statement in answer to the question: 'What is our reason for existence?' They are also likely to set the values for the organization – its duties and obligations to the various stakeholders (staff, customers, suppliers, the community) on which it depends.

These statements of mission and values are then passed down, with individual functions being asked to consider what they can achieve to deliver the mission, in line with the values. Of course, this is a messy process. It is likely to take several interactions before all the inconsistencies between functions have been resolved. Nevertheless, it does mean that the resulting plans will be realistic, achievable and consistent.

Motivation and co-ordination

There are two approaches to decision-making in any organization: procedures and values.

The first approach is centralized. It involves those at the centre working out all the decisions which colleagues in the line will be required to make and formalizing the form those decisions should take through books full of rules and procedures. Traditionally, this has been the approach taken by the Civil Service and retail businesses to achieve consistency.

CASE STUDY

Every outlet of the Waitrose supermarket chain has its own training room. Each room is lined with training materials specific to Waitrose. These deal with every issue, from how a till operator should give change, to how to deal with a suspect credit card, to how to calculate leave entitlement, to what to do in case of an out-of-hours break-in. Each situation is described in detail and a clear and detailed set of instructions given for handling it.

The alternative 'values' approach is epitomized by the IBM 'Blue Book'.

CASE STUDY

IBM, known traditionally as 'Big Blue' because of its corporate colours, publishes a slim pamphlet of organizational values. These are based on the principles followed by Thomas J. Watson, the company's founder. There were originally just three of them:

- Give full consideration to the individual employee
- Spend a lot of time making customers happy
- Go the last mile to do a thing right.

Over time, these three principles have been extended and formalized. Nevertheless, when faced with a difficult decision, it is to this slim pamphlet of values rather than to a manual of procedures that IBM executives turn.

This 'values' approach is in line with the philosophy of decentralization we have already discussed. From a motivation viewpoint, it allows people to adopt a proactive method of decision-making and thereby feel that they are a responsible member of the organization. In terms of co-ordination, it provides a simple and non-bureaucratic way of achieving and maintaining consistency. Nevertheless, the approach has its dangers. Organizational values are only meaningful if they are exemplified by behaviour as well as by being published. Values will only be understood and properly applied if they are modelled consistently by colleagues and managers.

ENVIRONMENTAL DEMANDS AND CONSTRAINTS

The strategic planning process we have already described starts with an analysis of the environment in which the organization operates. The management literature describes the factors to be considered as:

- political
- economic
- social
- technological
- legal
- environmental.

Political factors

Political actions and decisions may open or close markets, that is, make them less or more attractive. If you work for a not-for-profit organization, these actions may change your tax situation or influence the demand for your services. If, historically, yours has been a government operation or nationalized industry, political decisions may change your status.

Economic factors

The level of economic success, whether international, national or local, will influence:

- customer spending power
- the advisability of expansion
- the nature of demand
- the availability of funding
- the reward structure necessary to attract staff.

Social factors

Social changes may:

- increase or decrease your customer base
- change your customer profile and their requirements from you

- affect staff availability
- influence your physical distribution network.

Technological factors

Technology may:

- change the nature of your products and services
- increase or decrease the demand for them
- affect the way they are produced
- affect the way they are delivered
- influence their costs
- influence their value.

Legal factors

Legislation may impact on what your organization is allowed and not allowed to do. New legislation could change:

- working practices
- customer rights and expectations
- employee rights and expectations
- community rights and expectations.

Environmental factors

Interpreted as 'care for the physical environment', environmental influences affect a range of organizational considerations, including:

- the choice of raw materials
- manufacturing methods
- choices of physical distribution channels
- the format of packaging
- energy usage.

Depending on your place and responsibility in the operations management process and the sector in which you work, you may be called on to:

- assess the impact of a political decision
- implement a budget affected by political considerations
- increase or decrease production in line with market demands
- take account of social factors when recruiting staff
- implement or use new technology

- make technological changes to existing products
- implement new working practices as a result of changes to legal requirements
- change the raw materials you use or the way you dispose of waste
- achieve energy savings.

At the very least, you will find it helpful to understand the environmental considerations which have led to the decisions you are required to implement. At the other end of the scale, it may be part of your role to contribute to those decisions.

THE HIERARCHY OF DECISIONS

We have already stated the argument that operational decisions should be taken by people closest to the point of impact. However, this is another piece of management theory which is not always supported by organizational reality!

Referring to a more hierarchical approach to decision-making, Rosemary Stewart (*The Reality of Management*, Butterworth-Heinemnn, 1997) quotes research by the American academic Norman Martin. She explains:

Norman Martin looked at the different levels of management in a large American manufacturing company. He found that the decision situation differed in a number of ways between the levels. By 'decision situation' Martin meant the whole range from the preliminary stages, through the actual decision and implementation to verification of the correctness or incorrectness of the decision.

The main differences he discovered were in the length of the time perspective, the amount of continuity and the degree of uncertainty. Decisions at the higher levels have as one would expect a longer time perspective. From first inquiry to verification of the decision took less than two weeks in 97.7% of the shift foreman's decision situations; 68% of the department foreman's decision situations were completed within two weeks; 54.2% of the division superintendent's; and only 3.3% of the works manager's. Half of the works manager's decision situations lasted over a year; 4.3% of the division superintendent's, 1.5% of the department foreman's and none of the shift

---

foreman's. This shows the striking difference in distant-time perspective between the works manager and the other three levels of management. Decisions at the higher level tended to be discontinuous as one would expect with a long time span. There were sometimes wide gaps between the different parts of the decision situation, partly due to the manager having delegated part of the process of carrying through a decision to his subordinates. At the lower levels all the stages tend to follow each other without a time interval, or with only a short one.

The decisions at the lower levels were much more clear cut. What had to be done was more easily seen, it usually had to be done quickly and there was less uncertainty about the result than at higher levels. At the higher levels the decision situation was much more indefinite; the time within which action should be taken was often indeterminate as it would depend upon the judgement of the total situation; what should be done was often difficult to decide because there were so many elements of uncertainty in the decision.

It would be a mistake to place too much emphasis on the detail of this research. But it would equally be a mistake to overlook the broad findings it contains. In simple terms, these can be summarized as:

- High-level decisions take a long time to take, implement and evaluate.
- High-level decisions are discontinuous, with time gaps between the various stages.
- High-level decisions involve considerable uncertainty about the nature of the issue to be resolved and the likely success of the action decided on.

Those three points have significant implications for decision-making in operations management. When faced with an operational decision, ask yourself:

- How much do you know about the issue to be resolved?
  - What are the causes? Are you sure?
  - If not, who of your colleagues or subordinates could tell you more?
  - How complete is the evidence you currently have?

- What would an effective decision look like?
  - What must the solution achieve?
  - How would you measure success?
- What are the limits to your decision?
  - What are your limits of authority?
  - What other constraints limit your choice of solution? (For example, time, cost, resource availability, expertise, legal constraints)
- What alternative decisions or solutions are open to you?
  - How well would each satisfy the objectives an effective decision must achieve?
  - How far does each fit within the limits you have identified?
- If the decision exceeds your limits of authority, who is authorized to take it?
  - Your boss?
  - Another department?
- What evidence, information and guidance will they need?
  - About the issue?
  - About the alternatives?
  - About the risks?
  - About the necessary resources?
  - About the likely success of your proposed solution?
- Once the decision has been taken, how will you measure its success?
  - Has the issue been resolved?
  - How much did it cost?
  - How long did it take?
  - What resources did it consume?

We can summarize these questions in the form of the decision-making model shown in Figure 2.4.

You will notice that the model does not incorporate the referral of the problem to someone else in the organization. This is for two reasons. First, in line with the philosophy of delegated decision-making, we would prefer to believe that those who have recognized an issue will be given the authority to deal with it.

Secondly, we recognize that the reality of operational decision-making isn't always like that. As a consequence, we cannot be sure whether the culture of your organization will require you to refer an issue as soon as you have defined it. (Box 1 in Figure 2.4), or when you have recognized that it is outside your limits of authority (Box 3), or when you have identified some options (Box 4), or when you want agreement to implement a preferred solution (Box 5).

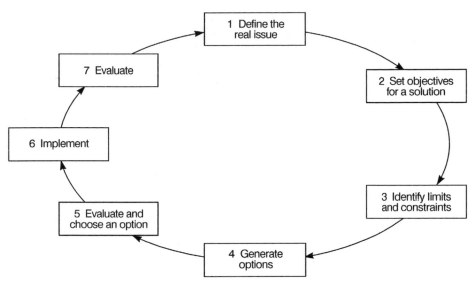

Figure 2.4 A model for decision-making

If you have the authority to deal with issues which affect you or your team, this problem does not apply. If, on the other hand, there are limits to the decisions you can take, it will be important for you to remember to present sound evidence and reliable information to whomever you want to support you.

COMPETENCE SELF-ASSESSMENT

1 Does your organization practise centralized or decentralized decision-making?
2 How consistent is that approach with staff and customer expectations, available expertise, the need for control and co-ordination?
3 How effectively does your organization control its operations?
4 How much do you know about your organization's strategy, mission and goals?
5 How would you find out more about them to be more effective in your job?
6 To what extent do environmental factors impact on the work you do?
7 How could you find out more about them?

8   What are your limits of decision-making authority?
9   Faced with a decision which exceeds your authority, who would you go to?
10   How persuasive have your arguments been in the past? And how could you improve them in the future?

3 Managing resources

In the Introduction to this book, we stressed the need for operations to be:

- effective – delivering the right product or service, one that meets the needs and wants of your customer, on time, every time
- efficient – using the fewest possible inputs to deliver the product or service to specification, keeping costs and waste to a minimum
- responsive – accommodating changes in political, economic, social, technological, legal and environmental factors, in the marketplace and in customer demand, in order to ensure that your product or service and the methods used to produce and deliver it are consistent with market needs and best practice.

To achieve these three criteria, it is necessary for the operations manager to control four key elements:

- physical capacity
- operating schedules
- inventory of both raw materials and finished stocks
- staff capability.

In this chapter, we will consider each of those four elements in turn.

MANAGING CAPACITY

Capacity levels

All operations have:

- an optimum capacity. This refers to the level of output which is consistent with efficient and economic running of the operation, whilst still allowing time for maintenance of the resources used. This may be physical maintenance of equipment and machinery, particularly in the case of a manufacturing operation, or the training and development of staff if the operation is heavily dependent on its people resource.
- a maximum capacity. This refers to the level of output which makes fullest use of all the resources required by the operation. When running at maximum capacity, an operation will have all its machinery running at full speed, with no time for any maintenance other than running repairs. Staff will be working as much overtime as they are prepared to work or as much as they can be allowed to work without falling ill or endangering their own safety or the quality of the output. Two very different case studies will illustrate this.

CASE STUDY

You may not naturally think of a battle as an operation! Nevertheless, a battle can be seen as the transformation of inputs – shells, troops, guns, expertise and experience – into a desired output: the defeat of the enemy. Commenting in his book *Gallipoli* (Wordsworth Editions, 1997) on the battle of Chunuk Bair during the First World War, Alan Moorhead describes the human causes of failure:

On both sides the men had been fighting for three days and nights without sleep, and with very little water or food. The trenches behind them were choked with dead and wounded, and most of those who were still living looked out on their hideous surroundings through a fog of exhaustion. They lay on the ground, they waited, and they responded to their orders like robots with dull mechanical movements.

A more current example comes from the National Health Service.

CASE STUDY

Junior doctors in the NHS are expected to spend extended periods working in hospitals' casualty departments. Until 1997, a typical week of duty exceeded 80 hours. The intention was that the week would be made up of alternating periods of work and time 'resting' but on call. However, because the flow of patients (which constitutes customer demand for a hospital) is so unpredictable, it was not unusual for casualty doctors to work 48 hours without sleep. The resulting misdiagnoses and occasional patient deaths have forced the NHS to reduce junior doctors' working week. Nevertheless, this is being achieved very slowly, because there are too few doctors on the payroll and coming into training.

Most operations also have a minimum capacity. This is the level of output at which the cost of the operation is at breakeven level. In other words, if the operation produced any less, it would be making a loss.

Managing operational capacity is a relatively straightforward process, provided that one of two situations applies:

- demand for the outputs (products or services) is consistent and predictable
- the operation is designed to achieve flexibility of response through simple adjustments to resource availability.

Neither of these situations arises naturally. However, several techniques and strategies exist to smooth demand and build in flexibility.

Smoothing demand

Demand for an operation's outputs depends on:

- the nature of overall demand for the product or service
- the level and quality of the competition
- the quality of the operation's own outputs
- pricing policy.

It helps understanding to separate the factors affecting demand in this way. However, the separation is an artificial one. For example:

- Overall demand will influence the level of competition.
- Quality of outputs should take account of the quality of competitors' outputs, as we shall see when we consider benchmarking in Chapter 4 of this book.
- Pricing policy is a consideration perceived by customers as an element of quality, or at least value for money.

If all these factors remained constant, then demand for the operation's outputs would be both consistent and predictable, and capacity could be planned and managed accordingly. However, in most operations, this is not the case. For example:

- With few exceptions, restaurants experience their greatest demand at lunchtime and in the evenings. But premises, furniture and kitchen equipment are all renewable or fixed resources, with associated costs which cannot be adjusted to match demand.
- Seaside hotels experience their greatest demand during the summer holiday period.
- The demand for barbecues is highest during the hot weather.

Actions to smooth demand may take one or more of five forms:

- differential pricing
- product or service diversification
- making to stock
- customer queuing
- encouraging customer loyalty.

Although these are largely different techniques, it is sometimes possible to enhance the effectiveness of one by combining with another, as we shall see.

Differential pricing

This is the best known technique for smoothing demand. It involves attracting customers at periods of low demand by offering price reductions and discounts.

QUESTION

What examples of differential pricing can you think of?

You may have come up with any of the following (some are more obvious than others):

- January and summer sales in the high street
- 'bargain break' holidays out of season
- 'off-peak' ticket prices on the railways
- evening and weekend price reductions for telephone calls
- 'off-peak' electricity for domestic heating
- higher night-time rates for taxi journeys
- commercial gas prices which favour manufacturing processes at night.

All of these approaches are intended to increase the usage of resources which would otherwise be underutilized. It is also worth noticing that the majority apply to service industries, where the processes involved do not allow the business concerned to 'make for stock' by producing now, then storing the product to meet later demand.

Differential pricing can also be combined with:

- customer queuing
- encouraging customer loyalty.

Customer queuing, as we shall see in more detail later, involves making customers wait for the product or service they want. However, most customers are unwilling to wait, unless they receive some tangible benefit.

CASE STUDY

Most airlines offer 'stand-by' flights. Under this arrangement, customers are expected to wait until a seat is available on an aeroplane to their desired destination. Airlines compensate for this inconvenience by offering stand-by flights at reduced prices. A further advantage, which is also an example of differential pricing, is that passengers may find themselves upgraded from one class to another. This further smooths demand by ensuring that all cabins on the plane are full.

There are several ways of encouraging customer loyalty, as we shall see. Very often, they are combined with differential pricing by offering customers a price benefit or bonus if they buy regularly from the same source.

J. Sainsbury, the supermarket, offers customers 'Reward cards'. These are a form of cash card, onto which the checkout operator registers a credit each time the customer makes a purchase. This approach smooths demand by discouraging customers from buying from the competition (Tesco, for example, or the local corner shop). It operates as differential pricing because customers can spend their Reward card credits as part or full payment for later purchases.

Product or service differentiation

This technique is primarily a response to seasonal fluctuations. It involves designing operation processes and, normally, multiskilling staff to take account of different levels of demand for different products and services at different times of year. You should be able to identify examples of product and service differentiation in manufacturing, service, commercial and not-for-profit operations.

QUESTION

What examples of product and service differentiation can you think of?

Here is a range of examples from a variety of sectors.

CASE STUDY

Manufacturing
Walls has been famous for ice-cream for many generations. However, ice-cream is most in demand during the summer. The reduced level of demand during the winter is compensated for at company level because Walls also make pies and sausages — both more popular during the cold weather.

Service

Local builders often offer external house redecoration during the summer — exterior paint does not dry well in the bad weather! — and internal painting and decorating during the winter. The skills required are not markedly different, so the same workforce is able to carry out both kinds of work.

Similarly, you may find that your local coal merchant delivers coal during the winter and offers a garden maintenance service during the summer.

Not-for-profit

Unfortunately, fires happen all the year round. However, there is a seasonal variation in the kinds that occur. In the winter, fires often involve chimney fires or misuse of heating appliances. In the summer, they are more likely to involve outdoor fires, for example from sparks alongside railway tracks, or picnic fires, or matches dropped on country walks. The Fire Service is equipped and trained to deal with both indoor and outdoor fires.

Making to stock

This technique smooths demand by manufacturing products at a fairly consistent level throughout the year, warehousing excess production when demand is low and supplying from stock when demand is high.

QUESTION

What types of product can you think of that are suited to this technique?

You may have mentioned:

- fireworks
- Christmas crackers
- frozen turkeys
- anti-freeze
- swimwear
- skis.

Many businesses combine making for stock with product diversification, thereby reducing costs by sharing the costs between products with different demand patterns, with the added benefit of maintaining turnover throughout the year.

CASE STUDY

W. H. Smith, the high street retailer, offers a wide diversity of merchandise from magazines to wrapping paper to pre-recorded and blank videos. Nevertheless, the company makes the whole of its profit during the months of November and December, as customers buy presents for Christmas. To cope with this huge upsurge in demand, W. H. Smith buyers start placing their Christmas orders in January. The merchandise starts arriving in the shops in July. Trading from January to October barely covers overheads, but is essential to survival. The Christmas rush can only be met by supplying from stock.

Customer queuing

As our definitions have already shown – and as Chapter 4 of this book will explore in more detail – effective operations management seeks to, amongst other things, produce the right products or services in the right quantities at the right time, in order to satisfy the customer. Making customers wait seems neither to deliver at the right time nor likely to achieve customer satisfaction.

However, there are exceptions to this rule. Some of these reflect the nature of customer demand, others bring benefits to the customer, some of which are obvious, some hidden.

CASE STUDY

Specialist car manufacturers (Rolls Royce, Mercedes, Morgan are good examples) regularly quote delivery lead times of two years or more for their vehicles. However, customers are happy to wait for delivery. A combination of clever marketing and tradition have persuaded actual and potential customers that only 'ordinary' cars are available off-the-shelf. In part, the delay emphasizes the fact that the car is being built to the customer's individual specification – in other words, that it is the result of a job or project operation. It also reflects the linkage in customers' minds between delay and quality, although that linkage is limited to only a few markets.

Indirectly, this case study also provides an example of the kinds of benefits which can persuade customers to queue. When a specialist car manufacturer like one of those mentioned above announces a new model – or even if the press spreads the rumour of a new model launch – the manufacturer will receive significant numbers of orders, regardless of the wait involved. For some of those 'early bird' customers the benefit will come from owning not just an exclusive make, but a rare, new model of that exclusive make, with the implications that has for social reputation.

For other 'early bird' customers, though, the benefit is more immediate and tangible. Because the new model is rare, it is highly sought after. Some purchasers of a new model buy it solely so that they can sell it on at a significant profit!

The next case study offers a more mundane example of a benefit which queuing can bring to the customer.

CASE STUDY

Fast food restaurants – whether Burger King, Kentucky Fried Chicken or your local fish and chip shop – will always have a price list, usually illustrated, displayed over the counter. There is often a bewildering choice. The time spent queuing allows customers to make their choice before reaching the counter, thus avoiding the embarrassment of not knowing what to ask for when they arrive.

Customers are becoming less willing to wait for the product or service they want. Whilst it is inarguable that resources are not cost-efficient if at any time there are no customers to benefit from them, this has to be balanced against the fact that long queues make customers impatient and likely to take their business to competitors – perhaps permanently. Consequently, organizations are increasingly sacrificing the cost-efficiency of customers waiting to higher standards of customer service.

CASE STUDY

Tesco now promises its customers that, if there are three people at all open checkouts, the supermarket will open another till. Of course, this has resource implications. Complaints that Tesco sometimes fails to honour its promise invariably result from a lack of available checkout operators.

Encouraging customer loyalty

We have already mentioned Sainsbury's Reward cards as one method of encouraging customer loyalty. Other, similar, retail examples are the popularity of Green Shield stamps in the 1960s and the extensive use of Argos Premier Points cards by BP petrol stations and other retailers. All these methods have the same objective: to offer customers an incentive to return regularly and consistently to the same supplier. Such loyalty schemes do not apply exclusively to retail operations.

QUESTION

What other methods can you think of to encourage customer loyalty?

You could have mentioned:

- season tickets for sports grounds or the railways
- members' enclosures at, for example, Henley and Ascot
- company boxes at theatrical or operatic first nights
- free wine with your meal at your second visit to a restaurant
- company loyalty discounts from hotel chains
- special contract terms for repeat business from just about every commercial supplier
- even the right, in the last century, to a named pew at the local church on payment of a one-off or annual sum by members of the gentry!

In all these examples, customer loyalty is repaid by discounted prices or added convenience. However, it will be obvious that customers will only remain loyal if their first experience of the organization was satisfying, of a high standard and met their needs. To take our extreme example, churchgoers would only have paid for a family pew if the sermon was interesting and the singing at least reasonable the first time they attended.

Which brings us to a recent initiative which encourages customer loyalty by enhancing customer satisfaction. This is the development of customer–supplier partnerships, to which we shall return in Chapter 4 in order to explore a further benefit they bring.

Customer–supplier partnerships work by abandoning the old practice of keeping customers at arm's length – where their role was to receive the product or service once it had been produced – in favour of involving customers at every stage of an operation. Customers will be involved in:

- product or service specification
- design
- development
- testing
- quality monitoring
- regular performance reviews
- revisions to the product or service.

In the context of customer loyalty, this approach brings benefits in the form of:

- a closer match between customer requirements and the output specification
- a reduction in complaints about quality or performance
- early warning of problems
- a greater feeling of ownership of the product or service on the part of the customer.

Evidence of customer–supplier partnerships often comes in the shape of joint working parties, regular consultation and focus groups, another topic we shall return to in Chapter 4.

Smoothing demand from internal customers

The examples and case studies we have quoted so far have all related to external or final customers. But it would be a mistake to assume that the techniques we have described do not apply to internal customers. We have mentioned methods related to:

- differential pricing
- product or service diversification
- making to stock

- customer queuing
- encouraging customer loyalty.

We have also pointed out that demand depends on:

- the nature of overall demand
- the competition
- quality
- price.

QUESTION

Bearing these issues in mind, which of the five techniques described earlier can be applied to internal customers?

You may be in the happy position of facing no competition at all for internal demand. If so, your customers will be forced to come to you, regardless of the quality you offer or how much it costs. You can make them wait as long as you choose, they can do nothing but remain loyal and you can confidently refuse to alter either the product or service you offer or the way you deliver it. Under those favourable circumstances, the only smoothing technique you need to worry about is customer queuing: 'If they want it, they'll have to wait'.

However, even under those circumstances, your internal customers still have some alternatives: they can do it themselves, or they can do without. Two case studies make the point.

CASE STUDY

Comment from an Operations Manager in a national charity:

We used to rely on Accounts to give us feedback on our income and expenditure. But they made such a mess of it, we decided we couldn't rely on them any more. So, we recruited our own Finance Officer. Now we know exactly how much money we have available and how much we have spent. Her information is reliable – the rubbish we got from Accounts never was.

> **CASE STUDY**
>
> The Training Manager of a national retail chain took the decision that management training should focus exclusively on interpersonal skills. Branch managers recognized the fact that management skills also included financial control, stock management and the legal aspects of staff discipline, amongst others.
>
> Demand for management courses dropped by 50 per cent in three years.

It is essential to note that, increasingly, organizations are moving away from the idea that internal customer–supplier relationships are fixed.

> **CASE STUDY**
>
> The 'Competing for Quality' initiative in government departments requires individual operations to be made subject to competitive tenders. Internal teams are entitled to bid, but their proposals and prices will be compared with those from external suppliers on the basis of:
>
> ■ fitness for purpose
> ■ quality standards
> ■ value for money.

As an internal supplier, therefore, you may find it a useful survival strategy to seek answers to the following questions:

■ Do the products or services I provide justify their costs to my customers?
■ Are there times when my operation could deliver at lower cost?
■ What additional products or services could I offer?
■ Are my team adequately multiskilled?
■ What could my operation be producing at times of low demand for our normal output?
■ Is there any way of storing our excess production?
■ In what ways could I turn waiting for my output into a benefit?

- Is the current delay in delivering my output acceptable to customers?
- What incentives – in the way of price, discount or convenience – do I offer for customer loyalty?
- How far do I operate in partnership with my customers?
- How could I operate more in partnership with my customers?
- How could I involve them more in output specification, design, development, testing, monitoring, review and revision?

Adjusting capacity

Regardless of the extent to which techniques are successful in smoothing demand, it will still, to some extent, remain inconsistent and unpredictable. Hence, the need to adjust capacity in line with demand. Such adjustments may involve major injections of capital at one extreme, to short-term remedial measures at the other.

Two techniques for adjusting capacity involve significant capital. A further four can be considered as short-term remedial measures, although the definition of short-term and remedial are relative.

Maintaining excess capacity

Our first technique for adjusting capacity runs counter to our argument that operations should make efficient use of resources. Strictly speaking, it may not even involve any adjustment to capacity. It certainly involves a major injection of capital. Simply, the technique is a question of forecasting peak demand and making resources available to meet it. A surprising number of operations apply this technique.

QUESTION

What examples of maintaining excess capacity can you think of?
How do they cope with the efficiency implications of this technique?

Here are a few examples:

- Holiday resorts maintain excess capacity in the shape of tourist attractions which remain underutilized during off-peak periods, but compensate for this by closing some

attractions out-of-season and encouraging joint marketing
initiatives to attract visitors at other times of the year.

■ The former USSR maintained excess capacity in the shape of
larger than necessary armed forces, but dealt with this by a
combination of charging high prices in the form of an
excessive proportion of Gross National Product and justify-
ing this through a strenuous propaganda programme.

■ Airlines maintain excess capacity by offering more seats
than necessary on many flights, but resolve the efficiency
implications by operating differential pricing.

Automation

Our second capital-intensive technique involves the adoption of automated,
frequently computer-controlled, operations. Typically, this technique brings
benefits in three ways:

■ Computer-controlled production allows more rapid adjustments to both the nature and volume of output.

■ Specifications for a range of outputs can be preprogrammed
and   stored,   thus   facilitating   product   or   service
diversification.

■ Automated operations release staff for other duties. Combined with the technique of multiskilling, which we shall
examine later, this allows staff to be used more flexibly.

CASE STUDY

The introduction of automated teller machines (ATMs),
known popularly as 'hole in the wall machines' or simply as
'cash dispensers', by the high street banks mean that
customers can draw cash, check account balances, request
statements or order cheque books at any time of the day or
night.

The range of services available from the machines is an
example of service diversification, whilst reducing staff
involvement simply to that of replenishing them. They are also
a response to changes in customer expectations from banking
and to changes in the social and technological environment.

As an operations manager, you are unlikely to have the authority to implement
either of these capital-intensive techniques without agreement from more senior

management. However, it is worth giving thought to the suitability of both maintaining excess capacity and increased automation to your operation – and the potential benefits – so that you can make a case for the introduction of one or both of them.

We shall now look at four techniques for adjusting capacity which concentrate on flexibility rather than capital. These are:

- flexible staffing
- multiskilling
- revising maintenance patterns
- subcontracting.

Flexible staffing

As the name suggests, this technique involves adjusting capacity by increasing or reducing staff numbers and/or hours worked.

QUESTION

How many different methods of flexible staffing can you think of?

Here is a fairly lengthy list of alternative approaches. Even so, it is not complete!

- *Overtime working.* This may be paid overtime, agreed between management and staff, or the normal expectation that professional and executive staff will work longer hours when the work demands it.
- *Annualized hours.* Instead of specifying how many hours staff are expected to work each week, some organizations have introduced specifications of annual hours. This means that employees work short hours during slack periods and long hours during busy ones. Although open to abuse if management makes unreasonable demands on staff, annualized hours can bring staff benefits in the form of extra holidays or time off at slack periods. These are more attractive, of course, if those slack periods coincide with decent weather!
- *Part-time working.* Introduced by public sector organizations largely in response to social change (an increase in women returners) and by retail organizations in response to

market patterns. Part-time working involves the negotiation of working patterns in line with the needs of both the job and the employee. For example, working hours may be full-time during school terms but none at all during school holidays; mid-morning till mid-afternoon; early morning till after lunch; before lunch till late afternoon.

The most flexible examples of part-time working come from retailing.

CASE STUDY

A typical demand pattern in a supermarket starts quietly first thing in the morning, becomes busy at lunchtime, quietens again mid-afternoon and reaches a peak late afternoon and into the evening. Superimposed on this is a weekly pattern, with Friday evenings and weekends busier than the rest of the week.

There are various part-time working responses to these patterns. Staff may work mid-morning to mid-afternoon, lunchtime to close of business, evenings only, Saturdays only, weekends only. Yet others will come in after the store closes to clean up and restock the shelves ready for the next day's opening.

- *Flexitime.* A precursor to annualized hours, flexitime typically allows staff to work so many hours less or more than their contract requires each week, provided that they meet the contract requirements over a one-, two-, or three-month period. Often seen (rightly) as a staff benefit, flexitime also enables the organization to adjust its operating capacity, provided that management–staff relations are harmonious enough for staff to be willing to accommodate the changing volumes of work.
- *Temporary shift-working.* Many manufacturing operations use temporary additional shifts in response to increases in demand. This may involve a temporary move from two-shift to three-shift working, or the short-term introduction of weekend shifts. Of course, this method is only truly flexible if the business has access to temporary staff in the area, whom they can call on at short notice.
- *Temporary, agency or contract staff.* Recent years have seen a major growth in agencies supplying temporary staff.

Temporary staff are no longer mainly clerical, secretarial or administrative. It is now possible to hire

- engineers
- accountants
- human resource managers
- Research and Development specialists
- project managers.

from agencies, all on a temporary basis.

An alternative is to hire staff on a short-term contract: three, six or twelve months. Indeed, organizations are increasingly turning all their employment contracts into fixed-term contracts: one, two or three years are typical.

- *'No work, no pay' contracts.* We have included this approach, not as one to be adopted, but by way of completeness. 'No work, no pay' contracts operate on the basis of recruiting and training staff, requiring them to be available, but only paying them if there is work. In its original form, this approach has been around for a long time. Many building firms used it for building labourers, who would arrive at the site first thing in the morning and stay to work if needed.

More recent examples are less humane. There have been several cases of fast-food catering staff expected to stay permanently on the employer's premises, but only being paid when there was an upturn in business. Whilst this new approach is more flexible for the organization than the traditional approach, we find it hard to justify from a human rights standpoint.

Multiskilling

This approach to adjusting capacity is simple in concept but significant in terms of its implications. The basic concept asserts that, if staff members are capable of carrying out a range of tasks, they can be moved to those tasks which are needed to satisfy customer demand.

CASE STUDY

The Civil Service promotes people into grades rather than specific jobs. The intention is that civil servants should receive training in a wide range of skills, so that they are capable of performing equally satisfactorily in, for example, a strategy

planning, contracts management, accounting or human
resources function.

You may see this intention as unrealistic. If so, you
would be right! Many civil servants express a wish to
specialize. To address this wish, two promotion systems now
apply in parallel. Individual jobs are advertised and staff can
achieve promotion by applying successfully for one of them.
At the same time, staff can also ask to attend a promotion
board, success at which gives them the necessary 'ticket' to
be posted to the next available job at the relevant grade.

This case study has several implications for multiskilling:

- Its success is dependent on the quality and potential of the
  staff.
- Its success is dependent on their willingness to take on a
  variety of tasks.
- Its success is dependent on the quality and availability of
  training in the various skills.

Revising maintenance patterns

A well-run operation will set aside time for regular maintenance of equipment
and updating or upgrading of staff skills. A way of adjusting capacity to demand
is to revise equipment maintenance and staff training schedules, bringing these
forward when demand is low and deferring them when demand is high.

Of course, the approach has dangers. Maintaining equipment too soon
or too frequently may simply be a waste of time, effort and resources. Deferring
maintenance for too long may result in expensive machine breakdown.

Equally, training people just because they have no work to do probably
means that they will have no chance to practise the new skills or knowledge they
have gained. And 'skills you don't use, you lose'. Deferring training is also
dangerous. In a busy work environment, there is never a good time to train staff.
As a result, training is not just deferred – it simply never happens!

Nevertheless, used intelligently, the practice of revising maintenance
patterns to suit demand offers valuable scope for flexibility.

Subcontracting

Our final method is often described as the 'make or buy' decision. When
demand is relatively light, operations are carried out in-house. When demand is
heavy, increased use is made of subcontractors.

The 'make or buy' title suggests that this technique applies primarily to manufacturing. This, however, is not the case. For example:

- A training organization can design its own materials in slack periods, but buy in generic materials or commission a consultant to design for them at busy times.
- The workshop in a garage may use an apprentice to take a customer to the bus stop in slack periods, but call a taxi at busy times.
- The ambulance service will transport outpatients in their own sitting-cars when these are available, but use volunteer drivers at other times.

Literature on operations management often states that using subcontractors gives them an opportunity to learn your trade secrets and skills and then set up in competition with you. Whilst this does happen, the risk can be minimized by careful wording of contracts. In any case, such action would run counter to most business ethics. The argument that such action would be unethical may not always be very powerful, but breaches of ethics will have a significant adverse effect on the subcontractor's chances of gaining work elsewhere.

QUESTION

Which of these remedial techniques could you make more use of:

- flexible staffing?
- multiskilling?
- revising maintenance pattern?
- subcontracting?

MANAGING OPERATING SCHEDULES

The process of operations scheduling sets out to ensure that the sequence of activities which make up an individual operation, and the sequence of operations which support and depend on each other, are logical and efficient. The ease with which the scheduling process can be carried out depends on:

- the complexity of the operation. The more stages or activities in an operation, the more scope there is for delays, waste and inefficiency.

- the duration of the operation. Long operations are more difficult to schedule, but give more opportunity to increase efficiency by rearranging the component activities.
- the nature of the operation. As we explained in the last chapter, operations may involve one-off jobs, batches or continuous flow. The more repetitive the operation, the more experience will be available with which to streamline it and enhance its efficiency.

Effective operations scheduling involves the analysis and planning of four key elements:

- activity duration
- activity frequency
- activity sequence
- activity timing.

Activity duration

Under this heading, it is necessary to consider:

- how long the activity takes to complete
- the resources currently used to complete it
- its impact on the next activity in the sequence.

In most, but not all cases, the time needed to complete an activity will depend on the resources used. For example:

- Two postmen should be able to complete a delivery round twice as fast as one.
- Calculations done on a calculator should be quicker than if done with paper and pencil.

CASE STUDY

B. F. Skinner, known as 'the father of scientific management', observed a team of workers shovelling coal. He noticed that, being casual workers, each man had brought his own shovel and that some performed work more efficiently than others. Skinner identified the most efficient shovel design, then bought and issued enough for all the team. Output improved dramatically.

This case study raises the issue of the suitability of the resources for the activity. This applies to both physical and human resources. It is worth asking yourself:

QUESTION

> Are the physical resources used by my people suitable for the job?

The answer may raise issues related to, for example:

- the comfort of the seating
- how effectively computer programs deal with specific tasks
- whether there are enough telephones to go round
- should the photocopier be upgraded to offer double-sided copies or a collation facility
- whether the containers used for component storage are big enough
- whether fork-lift trucks have a high enough reach
- whether delivery vehicles are too small for the size of load, or too big for customer's unloading bays.

QUESTION

> Do my people have the capability to do the job?

It is obvious that inexperienced staff are likely to be slower and more prone to error than experienced ones.

CASE STUDY

> When the Road Transport Industry Training Board were making a film about basic workshop practice, they asked an experienced fitter to demonstrate how to change a wheel. He did it so quickly that it was impossible to identify his actions. They had to find a recently qualified trainee to demonstrate the task instead!

Matching people to jobs is an essential process which we will cover in more detail later in this chapter.

As a result of asking such questions, it is always tempting to embark on a remedial or improvement programme. However, such action would be premature.

For the purpose of operations scheduling, it is necessary first to consider the impact of reducing the time taken by an activity on the next activity in the sequence. If speeding it up has no benefit, it is not worth doing. Equally, if the cost of improvement exceeds the efficiency savings gained, again it has no value. Whilst the theme of continuous improvement is attractive, it does not justify remedial action which achieves nothing, or is more costly than leaving things as they are.

Activity frequency

The more frequently an activity takes place, the more worthwhile it is to invest in making it more efficient. This is a fundamental principle of time and motion study, which involves experts with clipboards and stopwatches observing and analysing the actions which make up tasks, and the tasks which make up activities.

Failure to seek ways to make frequent activities more efficient leads to longer task durations, increased costs and, if they are physical activities, often to strain or injury.

CASE STUDY

The workplace injury known as RSI (repetitive strain injury) often affects wordprocessor operators. The cause most usually identified is that their workstations are designed for traditional typewriters, whilst the physical movements necessary to operate a wordprocessor are different and inconsistent with the layout provided for a typewriter.

Activity sequence

The analysis of activity sequence goes to the heart of operations scheduling. It involves critical examination of the whole chain of activities which make up an operation, in order to identify such inefficiencies as:

- double handling
- repetition

- time spent waiting
- excessive distance between activities.

CASE STUDY

The diabetic clinic of the Radcliffe Infirmary in Oxford is world-famous for the expertise of its consultants and the quality of treatment. A typical patient visit will include:

- a blood test
- an eye examination
- a foot examination
- a review of any problems since the last visit
- an interview with the consultant.

In order to improve the sequence of those activities, the clinic has introduced a new system:

- Patients go to their own GP for a blood sample to be taken.
- The sample is sent to the clinic in advance of the patient's visit, so that the results are already available when the patient arrives.
- A nurse examines the patient's eyes on his or her arrival at the clinic, during the time otherwise spent waiting to see the consultant.
- Patients are encouraged to keep a diary of events since their last visit in a set format, so that this information is readily available to the consultant.
- Feet are examined by a qualified podiatrist after the patient's interview with the consultant. The podiatrist then agrees and prescribes any necessary treatment, which is recorded in the patient's notes for later reference.

The implementation of this system has brought down typical attendance at the clinic from over an hour to twenty-five minutes.

The most common method of analysing activity sequence is by the use of a flow chart or network diagram. An example of a simple network diagram for the operation of carrying out an office removal is shown in Figure 3.1.

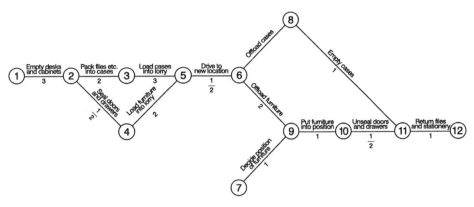

Figure 3.1   Network: office removal

The conventions of a network diagram are as follows:

- All activities start and finish with a circle (called a 'node').
- Nodes are numbered for ease of reference (there is no special logic to the numbering).
- Activities are described in action words above the line, with the duration below.
- Durations can be in anything suitable from seconds to weeks, as long as they are all consistent.
- 'Burst' nodes are points where several activities can start when one is completed.

Network diagrams have several advantages:

- They enable you to identify the sequence of activities which determine the minimum duration of an operation (the 'critical path' through the network).
- They encourage you to concentrate on improving those activities which can bring about real efficiency savings in an operation.
- They provide scope for streamlining an operation by identifying those activities which could be carried out in parallel.
- They highlight waiting time.

If you want to know more about the use of network diagrams, refer to the Institute of Management Foundation's Open Learning Text *Understanding Business Process Management* (Teresa Riley, Pergamon, 1997), which explains the process in greater detail and provides opportunities to practise.

Activity timing

So far, we have considered the duration, frequency and sequence of activities as existing in their own right. In other words, we have paid little attention to practical realities, like delivery dates specified in a customer contract, or the requirements of an internal customer.

However, analyses of activity duration and activity sequence will both contribute to decisions about activity timing. They can assist calculations of what timings are achievable and realistic, whilst knowledge of the timings can also assist with decisions about, for example, the need for efficiency savings or how many resources to allocate. For example:

- At several points in this book, we have stressed the need to deliver customer satisfaction. In job or project operations, in particular, it is tempting to attempt this by promising early delivery dates. However, nothing is more likely to lead to customer dissatisfaction than a missed delivery promise! Careful analysis of activity duration and activity sequence will ensure that the delivery promises you make are realistic.
- Alternatively, you may be required to achieve specified activity timings. Analyses of activity duration and sequence will enable you to work out whether your current processes make those timings achievable and, if not, what scope you have to shorten the overall operation by allocating extra resources, carrying out activities in parallel or achieving efficiency savings in individual activities.

MANAGING INVENTORY

Most operations depend on the careful management of inventory. In manufacturing operations, that dependence is obvious:

- Inputs arrive partly in the form of raw materials, components or subassemblies. The operation depends on their availability.
- Outputs take the form of finished goods, which in most cases will need to be warehoused prior to delivery to the final customer. Too much money tied up in finished stock is a heavy financial drain on the business.

The relevance of inventory management to service operations is less obvious. However, some simple examples will make the relevance clear:

- Schools depend on paper, textbooks, chalk, paint for art classes.
- Hospitals depend on syringes, blood, swabs, nurses' uniforms, clean bedlinen.
- Garage workshops depend on spare parts, oil, anti-freeze.
- Theatres depend on costumes, tickets, refreshments, scenery.
- Cleaning contractors depend on disinfectant, polish, dusters, invoice pads.
- The importance of inventory to retail outlets goes without saying!

Inventory is a necessary evil. Held at too low a level, items are likely to run out, which halts production and leaves an operation without saleable output. And it is irrelevant whether the out-of-stock item is a major or minor one. The result is the same.

CASE STUDY

When Reliant, the manufacturer of three-wheeled cars, returned to production after a period in the hands of the receiver, unfinished bodies and components to make engines were still available in the factory. This did not prevent a delay of three weeks, because the purchasing staff were unable to find a supplier of headlamp bulbs who was willing to supply a commercially risky customer.

At the same time, excess inventory is expensive. It is likely to deteriorate, may become obsolete and requires costly storage. It is therefore necessary to walk a very narrow line between inadequate and excess inventory, in order to maintain an inventory buffer which is sufficient to keep an operation running without prejudicing its cost-efficiency.

Three activities are central to effective inventory management:

- forecasting demand
- controlling stock
- replenishing stock.

Forecasting demand

Demand forecasting as it relates to inventory takes place at both a macro and a micro level. It also takes account of both quantitative and qualitative elements.

At a macro level, demand forecasting is part of strategic marketing. It analyses the environmental factors described in Chapter 2 to identify future customer needs and wants, competitive pressures and overall changes in the nature of the market. This is largely a qualitative analysis, although organizations will use as much quantitative data – in the shape of research reports, government and trade statistics and available past sales records.

It is easiest to picture this process as it relates to external markets and customers, but it is equally relevant to internal customers. Changes in your internal customers' processes or operations will change what they expect from you. Customer departments may increase or decrease the scale of their operation, thus affecting the size of their demand on you. And, as we explained earlier in this chapter, the opportunities for traditional internal customers to go to external suppliers are growing.

At a micro level, demand forecasting seeks to establish, with as much accuracy as possible, future demand patterns on a daily, weekly and monthly basis. In continuous operations, it may even be necessary to forecast demand on an hourly basis!

Micro forecasting is heavily dependent on quantitative techniques. After all, inventory management is fundamentally a matter of having the right items, in the right quantities, in the right place, at the right time. Consequently, demand forecasts with a wide margin for error run major risks of holding excess inventory, or running out of stock. However, as we shall see later, when we examine stock control methods, there are some categories of item where it is preferable to hold large buffer stocks.

Fortunately, short-term demand forecasting at a micro level can be carried out with greater accuracy than long-term strategic forecasting. At a micro level, demand forecasting typically makes use of three techniques.

Extrapolation from historical data

This involves a combination of time series and trend analysis and the use of moving averages. Consider the following example.

COMPETENCE SELF-ASSESSMENT

The Office Manager of Excel Engineering is responsible for several operations. One of these is the production of customer invoices and statements. Both are raised on specially printed, headed documents. Here are some details of the numbers of invoices and statements raised weekly in the past three months, with some supporting data from last year.

This year

Month	1				2				3			
Week	1	2	3	4	1	2	3	4	1	2	3	4
Invoices	7	7	9	11	8	9	11	13	9	9	13	13
Statements	0	0	0	20	0	0	0	24	0	0	0	26

Last year

Month	1				2				3			
Week	1	2	3	4	1	2	3	4	1	2	3	4
Invoices	6	6	8	10	7	8	10	12	8	8	12	12
Statements	0	0	0	18	0	0	0	22	0	0	0	24

It is now the end of month 3. How many invoices and statements should the Office Manager expect to raise in each of the four weeks of month 4?

A comparison of this year's and last year's figures show some clear trends:

- Statements are all raised in the last week of the month.
- More invoices are raised in weeks 3 and 4 of each month than in the previous two.
- The volume of invoices and statements is slightly higher this year than last year.

If we look at this year's figures alone, it looks as though they are following a rising trend. This would tempt us to predict month 4's invoices at around 10 in each of weeks 1 and 2, and around 14 in weeks 3 and 4, with perhaps 28 statements in week 4.

However, a comparison with last year's figures shows a marked seasonal pattern. Volumes drop significantly in month 4. Although we do not have enough data to be certain, it looks likely that the volumes for month 4 this year will be:

Month	4			
Week	1	2	3	4
Invoices	5	6	6	8
Statements	0	0	0	14

Historical data is accurate – it records what actually happened. Forecasts can be extrapolated from historical data by techniques from one extreme of scanning for a pattern – as we have just done – to complex computer programs, which quantify trends, at the other. But, as we know, history rarely repeats itself – or not exactly, anyway – which brings us to our second technique.

Quantitative prediction

We have already referred to the contribution of market research to demand forecasting and will return to the theme in Chapter 4. Fortunately for short-term forecasting, customers have a much better idea of their buying intentions in the short term than in the long term. For example, if you were asked where you were going to eat lunch today, you would have a much clearer idea than if you were asked where you were going to eat lunch on the same day, three months hence.

Consequently, quantitative prediction of short-term demand can, in many cases, involve customers. Weekly internal production meetings, involving both customers and suppliers, are an effective way of predicting next week's demand.

CASE STUDY

Rank Xerox operates a chain of in-house reproduction facilities on customers' premises. Each week, the manager of the facility asks customers for the volume and type of

reprographic work they will require the following week. The
written responses are received on Thursday and form the
basis for work scheduling and inventory management for the
next week.

Many services – restaurant tables, hotel rooms, airline seats – are booked in
advance. Pre-bookings offer another method of quantitative demand prediction.
Of course, they are not wholly accurate. Most airlines overbook in order to
maintain demand in the face of 'no shows'. Hotels, in particular, ask for a faxed
confirmation or credit card details when a guest books by phone. Nevertheless,
customer information is a reasonably accurate way of predicting short-term
demand.

Our last technique is far less reliable, but offers an important balance to
quantitative methods, which may be so dependent on numbers that they lose
sight of wider trends.

Qualitative judgement

Simply expressed, qualitative judgement uses informed judgement – 'gut feel' or
'inspired guesswork' – to predict demand. Although more often used in the
context of macro forecasting, there are situations where it is relevant to shorter-
term forecasting as well:

- The launch of a new product or service, where there is no
  historical data.
- Following a change in organization structure, where internal
  demands will come from new customers or differently
  structured departments.

QUESTION

Which of these three techniques could you make more use
of:

- extrapolation from historical data?
- quantitative prediction, using customer information?
- qualitative judgement, using hunches from experts or
  those with experience?

Controlling stock

Effective stock control demands answers to three questions:

- What stock do we have?
- What stock will we need?
- What is its value?

What stock do we have?

Unlikely as it may seem, it is often difficult for an organization, or even an individual operation, to determine just what inventory it is currently holding. In some cases, the problem is unavoidable. In others, it is the result of a systems failure. For example:

- In most organizations, separate departments hold their own stocks of printed stationery. Thus, one department may run out and order more, while the next department down the corridor has enough for several months – even years!
- Mobile repair engineers carry their own van-stocks of consumable items and replacement parts. For their own convenience, they normally carry excess stock. Put together, these excess stocks can be worth up to several thousand pounds.

A major cause is often a mismatch between stock records and physical stock, as this next case study shows.

CASE STUDY

When Toyota (GB) Limited introduced a computerized stock control system for vehicle parts, this incorporated a sophisticated program to reorder parts from Japan, but only when the stock of that part reached a specified level. In the early days, there were numerous cases where the warehouse pickers returned a picking-list marked 'out of stock', but the computer would not allow an order on the factory because its records showed that stock was available in the warehouse. In most cases, this resulted either from an inputting error, or because the stock had been put away in the wrong place in the warehouse.

Most organizations dread the thought of the annual stocktake. Nevertheless, this is not only a requirement for the preparation of the organization's balance sheet, it is also, for many, the only way of discovering just what stock they hold – and where it is. In view of this, it is not surprising that physical stocktaking now takes place, in some organizations, as often as once a month.

What stock will we need?

Part of the answer to this question comes from the demand forecasting process we have already examined. Another part of the answer comes from a careful analysis of all the inputs needed to achieve a given volume of output to job operations.

Continuous operations, if properly controlled, should generate a large amount of reliable historical data relating to the usage of raw materials, components, subassemblies, and consumables such as lubricants and cleansers. Effective data will also identify the split between inputs used and waste, with a view to improving cost control.

Batch operations should generate similar data. However, because these involve the production of a diverse range of outputs, less data will be available for individual outputs and, in addition, it will be more difficult to allocate common inputs to separate outputs. For example, if a photocopier is used by several teams, how much toner should be allocated as an input to the work of each?

Because job operations are unique, historical data will be unreliable. Comparisons with other jobs can be made, but these can only be approximate. With job operations, the prediction of required stock will be heavily dependent on the best estimates of those using it – another form of qualitative judgement.

The more careful the input analysis, the more reliable the historical data and the more expert the qualitative judgement, so the more likely it is that the operations manager will be able to predict the levels of stock required to achieve specified outputs.

What is value?

In any management process, the point comes where the cost of solving a problem is higher than that involved in leaving it alone. This definitely applies to stock control. Where inventory items are of high value, it is essential to monitor usage and waste very closely and to keep stock levels to the minimum required to achieve delivery of the output.

CASE STUDY

When W. H. Smith sold cameras and computers, these stocks were held in retail branches in small quantities and in a locked area of the stockroom. Only staff of management grade had access to these locked areas.

Low-cost items, on the other hand, will, if controlled too tightly, cost more to control than to buy!

Several alternative approaches exist to analyse inventory or stock values. However, they are all derived from the same basic principle, which is known as Pareto's Law. Pareto was a nineteenth-century Italian economist. His research into the population of Florence identified that 80 per cent of the wealth was owned by 20 per cent of the population. This '80:20 rule' has since been developed and applied to a wide variety of business and economic situations. For example:

- 80 per cent of sales come from 20 per cent of customers
- 20 per cent of staff cause 80 per cent of problems
- 20 per cent of customers make 80 per cent of complaints.

As it applies to inventory management, Pareto's Law is an encouragement to identify the small number of high-value items which represent the largest proportion of total stock value.

Because this application of Pareto's Law is a long way from nineteenth-century wealth distribution in Florence, it is unlikely that the analysis will show up a precise 80:20 distribution. However, the modern variation of Pareto's approach – known as ABC analysis – typically reveals some quite close approximations.

ABC analysis takes each inventory item, identifies its cost and turnover, then multiplies these to calculate its annual value. If items are then ranked in order of turnover value, a pattern something like that in Figure 3.2 typically emerges.

As Figure 3.2 shows:

- The most valuable 10 per cent of items account for 75 per cent of total annual turnover.
- The least valuable 75 per cent of items account for 10 per cent of total annual turnover.

The normal outcome of an ABC analysis is to develop a tight system of stock control for Class A items, a less sophisticated system for Class B items and, for Class C items, a system which controls stock by package or container load, rather than individually.

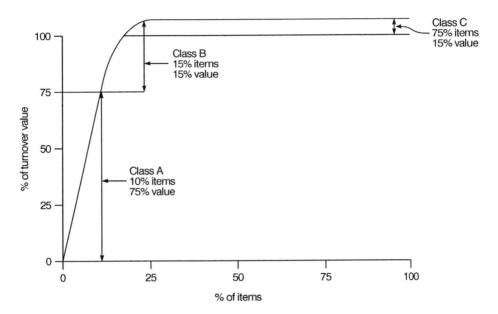

Figure 3.2   ABC analysis

Replenishing stock

Stock is a buffer between variations in demand and lack of availability of inputs. But holding stock is costly and inefficient. As a result, approaches to stock replenishment seek to keep stocks and costs to a minimum, whilst maintaining output.

The most recent development in replenishing stock is, strictly speaking, nothing to do with stockholding. Instead, Just-In-Time (JIT) techniques are designed to deliver inputs at precisely the time they are needed to be transformed into outputs. Looked at in one way, JIT has been around for a long time – as a way of delivering utilities. Gas, water and electricity are available to the consumer at the turn of a tap or by pressing a switch. Contrast gas central-heating, for example, where the gas is available on demand when the customer wants it, with oil-fired central heating, where oil supplies need to be ordered in advance and held in stock by the customer until required.

In a manufacturing context, JIT depends on the ability on the part of both customer and supplier to maintain a balance between the stability of the customer's requirements and the flexibility of the supplier's operating systems. If the customer's operation is continuous and stable, it is more likely that the supplier will be able to meet this regular and consistent demand on a JIT basis.

However, JIT is really an operational philosophy rather than simply a method of stock replenishment. It sets out to turn an operation into a continuous process or a seamless web. The implementation of JIT is likely to involve:

- a review of system design and layout to eliminate waiting, bottlenecks and transfer problems
- a close examination of activity sequences and durations to ensure that the speed and position of each activity are consistent with the operation as a whole
- a sophisticated system to call up inputs
- quality initiatives to eliminate defective inputs
- rationalizing product or service range, making greater use of shared components
- the design of maintenance programmes (equipment and people) to eliminate breakdowns and interruption
- multiskilling
- a commitment to continuous improvement
- increased customer–supplier co-operation in systems design, specification of requirements, timing, quantity and quality.

QUESTION

Is there any scope for JIT methods in your operation?

If JIT is not for you, your approach to stock replenishment will need to balance three factors:

- the cost of holding stock
- the cost of ordering stock
- the risks and consequences of stock-outs.

CASE STUDY

When garage workshops order parts, they normally have a choice between:

- monthly orders
- weekly orders
- vehicle-off-road (VOR) orders.

Monthly orders involve large quantities, a long wait, but 35 per cent discount. Weekly orders can be smaller, take less

> time, but the discount falls to 25 per cent. Vehicle-off-road orders can be for individual items, have a promised delivery of 24 or 48 hours but only 15 per cent discount.

If the cost of holding stock is high (either because the item is of high value or storage is expensive, for example, in an Oxford Street store), then the customer may do better to order smaller quantities more frequently.

However, if the ordering system is complicated or time-consuming (for example, involving a physical stock check, raising of a handwritten order which is then typed and sent to the supplier, with the consequent checking of stock on delivery and initiating of a manual payment process), it may be preferable to raise large orders infrequently.

And, of course, if stock-outs have costly consequences, it will be necessary to set high safety stock levels in order to satisfy 'worst case' demands.

MANAGING CAPABILITY

To finish this chapter, we will look briefly at the issue of staff capability, although we shall reserve a more detailed examination of the topic until Chapter 10.

A traditional organization employed two classes of people: managers and workers. Managers did the thinking and gave orders. Workers did as they were told. If this sounds like a Victorian hierarchy, it is worth recognizing that it was a typical approach in UK manufacturing until well into the 1960s. Indeed, you may also recognize the 'power culture', which Charles Handy identifies as characterizing owner-managed businesses and which we describe more fully in Chapter 4.

By contrast, we have already referred in this chapter to multiskilling and the philosophy of involving staff in continuous improvement; monitoring performance and managing change will become evident later in this book.

Nevertheless, it is important to make four points:

■ Managers can delegate authority but not responsibility. Involving your staff in decisions will necessitate giving them authority to take these decisions. But remember, if things go wrong – you are still responsible!

■ Not all staff want to be involved. 'That's not my job' or 'that's not what I'm paid for' are valid and understandable responses from staff who were not recruited, and until now have not been expected, to take part in operations management. Managing fear, resentment or abrupt changes in expectations requires considerable time, effort and care.

- Capability is not innate. Most people have the potential to achieve more than they are currently capable of. Nevertheless, changing potential into capability requires communication, training, support and encouragement, as we shall see in Chapter 10.

- People are different. Optimum performance varies between individuals. Assuming that all members of staff can reach the same standard is equivalent to assuming that all cars can reach the same top speed! Successful operations management involves assessing individual intelligence, skill, attitude and experience – and allocating tasks accordingly, in order to avoid 'square pegs in round holes'.

The process of managing capability therefore requires answers to the following questions:

- Am I recruiting the right staff for the jobs that need doing?
- How can I achieve the best match between tasks and individuals?
- What individual and/or group training do people need?
- How are the people needs of my operation changing?
- What must I do to accommodate those changes?
- Must I change the operation?
- Or can I change the people?

COMPETENCE SELF-ASSESSMENT

1   How effective, efficient and responsive is your operation?

2   Against which of these criteria is the shortfall greatest? How can you improve it?

3   How close is your operation to maximum capacity? What risks does this bring?

4   What more could you do to smooth demand from your customers?

5   What more could you do to adjust capacity to match demand?

6   Are the physical resources used by your staff suited to the work they do? What changes would you make?

7   Map the activity sequence of your operation. Where is there room for improvement?

8   How could you improve the accuracy of demand forecasting for your operation?

9   What are the drawbacks of your stock control systems? How could you overcome them?

10   How capable are your people of delivering your operation? What changes could you make?

4 The voice of the customer

Let's go back to the debate we were overhearing in Chapter 1. You will remember that it involved representations of finance, marketing, personnel and operations. We'll start with the marketing manager this time.

'Customers?' said the marketing manager. 'That's easy for me. They're the punters out there in the street. The ones who pay their hard-earned money for the products we make. Lovely people, all of them. Fickle, unreliable, always ready to complain – but lovely, all the same. After all they're the ones who pay our wages. Of course, I agree that it's the customers who make our lives difficult. Unreasonable demands. Always looking for a better or cheaper product somewhere else. But, let's face facts. Without customers, we go bust. Love them or hate them, we can't survive without customers. How about you, Mr Numbers?'

'We don't have customers', answered the accountant. 'Our job is quite different. We have a policing role. Sure, sometimes we have to bring in the money. But mainly our job is to make sure that you lot make good use of the resources you have. And, believe me, most of the time you don't! Sales below budget, overspends, underproduction. Where would you be if we didn't screw things down tight?'

'That's not the way I see things', asserted the personnel officer. 'Our job is to look after the people. We owe it to our staff to make sure they're treated fairly – not discriminated against, rewarded properly for the work they do, offered opportunities to develop, that sort of thing. The staff – they are our customers.'

The production supervisor was in a quandary. Like the marketing manager, he saw the buying public as his customers. But how could two functions in the same organization have the same customers? And, if the buying public weren't his customers, who were?

EXTERNAL AND INTERNAL CUSTOMERS

Focus on the external customer

You have no doubt already recognized the false assumptions and misapprehensions in this debate. But they are fundamental enough to be worth emphasizing.

The marketing manager takes a rather disparaging view of external customers. Essential they may be, but also fickle, unreliable and always ready to complain. He seems to accept the truth of the old joke often heard in retailing, that: 'This would be a wonderful place to work if it weren't for the customers'.

Of course, it is difficult to argue with the reality of the marketing manager's position. Evidence is widely available across all sectors of industry:

- The manufacturing customer who brings the date forward, then complains when the product is late.
- The retail customer who complains that the shop was shut at 5.31, when closing time is 5.30.
- The local government customer who refuses to pay council tax, but then protests at the state of the roads.
- The hospital patient who expects to be cured, but refuses to follow their course of treatment.
- The parent whose child always plays truant, but still expects him to pass his exams and blames the school when he or she fails.

So what should be the attitude of an organization towards its external customers? The answer to this question is a matter of perception.

Increasingly, organizations are coming to recognize that customers have rights and that the organization has duties towards them. This recognition can often be seen in the development and publication of a 'customer charter'. Here is an example, drawn from a business making home entertainment equipment:

Our aim is to provide our customers with high-quality, reliable and innovative products which will give long and satisfactory service.

Customers are the life-blood of our business. Their satisfaction is the focus of all our activity.

Customers have the right to expect the best possible service and we will always strive to give it.

We welcome customer complaints. Customers who complain are giving us the opportunity to put things right and improve our service.

All complaints will receive a written response within 24 hours.

All our products are guaranteed unconditionally for two years from purchase.

We will seek regular feedback from customers on all aspects of the service they receive.

This charter contains few surprises. It contains references to:

- product quality
- customer satisfaction
- customer service
- continuous improvement.

All of these references should be familiar as central themes of operations management.

On the other hand, if you are as cynical as most about local or national government, you may be surprised at the number of government departments which are now publishing their own customer charters. For example, you may have come across:

- patient's charter
- elector's rights
- taxpayer's charter.

In view of the traditional tension between taxpayers and the Inland Revenue, you may well not have expected the last, but here it is:

The Taxpayer's Charter

You are entitled to expect the Inland Revenue

To be fair

- by settling your tax affairs impartially
- by expecting you to pay only what is due under the law
- by treating everyone with equal fairness.

To help you

- to get your tax affairs right
- to understand your rights and obligations
- by providing clear leaflets and forms
- by giving you information and assistance at our enquiry office
- by being courteous at all times.

To provide an efficient service

- by settling your tax affairs promptly and accurately
- by keeping your tax affairs strictly confidential
- by using the information you give us only as allowed by the law
- by keeping to a minimum your cost of complying with the law
- by keeping our costs down.

To be accountable for what we do

- by setting standards for ourselves and publishing how we will live up to them.

If you are not satisfied

- we will tell you exactly how to complain
- you can ask for your tax affairs to be looked at again
- you can appeal to an independent tribunal
- your MP can refer your complaint to the Ombudsman.

In return, we need you

- to be honest
- to give us accurate information
- to pay your taxes on time.

Both the charters we have quoted are impressive, at least on the surface. They give guarantees and make promises. They offer benefits which should be attractive to most, if not all, of both organizations' customers. But, if you look critically at them, they ought to raise doubts in your mind.

QUESTION

What doubts do you have about the customer charters you have just looked at?

When considering a customer charter and the promises it makes about customer satisfaction and service, it is advisable to ask:

- How many people in the organization know what the document says?
- Do they understand its implications for the actions and decisions they should take?
- Has the organization worked out what it means by such promises as 'all our products are guaranteed unconditionally' or 'settling your tax affairs promptly and accurately'?
- Are effective systems in place to, for example, 'respond to complaints within 24 hours' or to 'give information and assistance at our enquiry office'?
- Does the charter genuinely reflect the values of the organization and the way people behave?
- Or is it no more than a paper exercise?

Despite the need to ask such questions on a regular basis, it is apparent that the proliferation of customer charters reflects a change in the relationship between supplier and customer – from one of conflict and confrontation to one of mutual dependence. The following extract is taken from an internal training publication by the Ministry of Defence, written for staff who manage contractors:

The way we feel about contractors will depend to a large extent on the experience we have had of working with them. For some MoD staff, contractors will be seen as unreliable, untrustworthy, out for a quick buck and never likely to give adequate service. In other words, contractors are the enemy and should be treated as such.

For others, who have had more positive experience, contractors are a valued source of specialist products and services, who can be relied on to deliver quality, on time and to cost. They are essential allies, colleagues in an effective partnership ... If you see them as enemies – people who can't be trusted – then your relationship with contractors will make it impossible for either of you to perform effectively.

From *Managing Contractors* © Crown Copyright. Published by the MoD, 1995

We shall return to this theme of the customer–supplier relationship as a partnership later in this chapter.

Focus on the internal customer

A further misapprehension from our earlier debate, which all four speakers are guilty of, is that of concentrating exclusively on external customers. This is a theme we introduced in Chapter 1. But it is worth developing further.

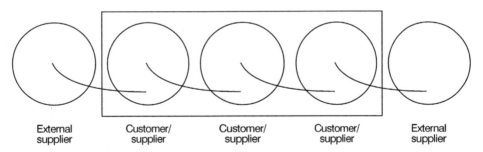

| External supplier | Customer/ supplier | Customer/ supplier | Customer/ supplier | External supplier |

Figure 4.1   The quality chain

It is convenient and helpful to picture an organization's customer–supplier relationship as a long chain, each link supplying the next one along the chain. You will find diagrams similar to the one in Figure 4.1 in most textbooks dealing with total quality management, which is where the concept of internal customers comes from.

Although the simple diagram in Figure 4.1 helps to get across a principle which is strange to many people, its simplicity leads to a distortion of the internal customer concept.

As John S. Oakland points out in his book *Total Quality Management* (Butterworth-Heinemann, 1989):

> Within organizations, between internal customers and suppliers, the transfer of information regarding requirements frequently varies from poor to totally absent. How many executives really bother to find out what their customers – their secretaries' – requirements are? Can their handwriting be read; do they leave clear instructions; do the secretaries always know where the boss is? Equally, do the secretaries establish what the bosses need – error-free typing, clear messages, a tidy office?

At this stage, the important point to be drawn from the quote is not the one related to customer requirements: this is so significant that we shall need to return to it in much more detail later in this chapter. Rather, it is the initially perplexing idea that one person can be both customer and supplier at the same time. We can identify some other examples, beyond Oakland's, of boss and secretary:

- In a project or job operation, every product and service is unique: a one-off. So the salesman needs to supply production with a clear and accurate statement of the external customer's requirements. But the salesman is also responsible for maintaining good relations with the external customer. So he is also the internal customer for the quality and effectiveness of the product or service, because these will have a major impact on customer relations.
- Every manager has a duty to supply subordinates with clear instructions and effective supervision, to be responsive to their needs and aspirations. At the same time, the manager is the customer for high-quality work, subordinates' productivity and routine but essential things like good time-keeping and attention to detail.
- In our debate, the accountant emphasized the policing function of the finance department. But that is also a two-way street. The finance department supplies financial and budgeting information to other departments. But, to do this, finance is dependent on them for the provision of raw data.

Further thought about this confused question of who are customers and who are suppliers goes a long way to dealing with the issue raised in the production supervisor's mind during our debate – about whether he or the marketing department supplied external customers.

The reality is that every department and individual in an organization is both supplier and customer to a host of other departments and individuals. The following case study makes this clear.

CASE STUDY

Until the mid-1990s, W. H. Smith operated a residential training centre at Milton Hill in Oxfordshire. Trainers were responsible for supplying:

- competent staff to the managers who sent them for training
- a stimulating and informative experience to delegates
- disciplined and effective programmes to their own managers.

At the same time, trainers had a right to expect:

- to receive, from the sending managers, delegates who wanted to learn
- co-operation and active involvement from the delegates
- training in how to do the job from their own manager
- good catering and comfortable accommodation (to keep delegates happy!) from the housekeeping staff.

OPERATIONS AS A HORIZONTAL PROCESS

Customer–supplier relationships

As the previous case study demonstrates, customer–supplier relationships are difficult to formalize, often operate across functions, take little or no account of hierarchical reporting structures and – at the same time – are essential to quality in operations management!

The messiness of this picture stems from two factors:

- our attempt to apply management theory to organizational reality
- the fact that we have been considering operations at a micro level.

Both factors are worth considering in more detail. Management theory sets out to explore:

- what does happen in organizations
- what should happen in organizations
- what might happen in organizations.

It is derived from:

- research
- direct experience
- the author's interpretation
- the author's prejudices.

It is also based in one moment of time – a snapshot of current events, if you like.

Consequently, in 1776 Adam Smith, writing in *The Wealth of Nations* (Penguin, 1986), asserted: 'The division of labour, however, so far as it can be introduced, occasions, in every art, a proportionable increase of the productive powers of labour.'

Whereas in 1976, Charles Handy, in his book, *Understanding Organizations* (Penguin, 1987), wrote: 'Organizations would, therefore, be well-advised to take the monotony out of jobs, for monotony is costly. To reduce men to extensions of machines cannot ultimately be right or profitable.'

- The implication of this is obvious – and totally consistent with the role of the manager. It is that operational improvements must be in line with the reality of the organization, its maturity, its people, its profitability and its technology. And, by extension: be careful to assess the fit of management theory with your organization before trying to implement it.

Our second factor is no more important, but it will take longer to develop. At a micro level, the analysis of who supplies whom – and with what, and to what standard – is an essential process, because of its impact on the efficiency of customer departments and on the quality of relations between departments.

CASE STUDY

A manager interviewed as part of a human resources audit in an environmental regeneration charity commented: 'Teams here don't support each other. Our relations with one other team are so dire we don't trust them at all any more. Instead of going to them for help, we do for ourselves the work they're supposed to do for us.'

At the same time, the analysis results in a web of customer–supplier transactions which, as an overall picture, may become so complex that it is almost impossible to unravel.

That is why it is important to keep clearly in mind the definition of operations at a macro level which we gave earlier in this book:

---

operations involves adding value through the transformation of inputs into outputs.

This transformation may involve:

- a change in form
- a change in content
- a change in location
- a change in size
- a change in presentation
- a change in reliability
- a change in efficiency.

The extent to which such transformations add value depends on how far they deliver to customers the benefits those customers are expecting. While this point may seem obvious, there are several significant obstacles to the successful achievement of added value:

- failure to recognize who are customers
- ignorance of their needs and expectations
- geographical separation
- bureaucratic or hierarchical separation.

It is for this reason that we have called operations a 'horizontal process'.

Organization structure and culture

Despite recent efforts by organizations to achieve looser, flatter structures based on co-operation rather than formality, most organizations continue to show evidence of functional separation, reinforced by hierarchies.

Charles Handy explained this phenomenon, and the problems arising from it, in his book *The Gods of Management* (Penguin, 1979). The book identifies four organizational structures or cultures, each named rather whimsically after a Greek god.

Handy's 'power culture' is named for Zeus, the god of thunderbolts and showers of gold. It describes an organization where all decisions are taken by the boss or a very small group of senior managers. The organization is quick to respond, tightly controlled, but only suited to small businesses.

The task culture is job or project orientated. Teams communicate and work together informally. They often split up and re-form as the needs of the task or project change. Respect is based on individual expertise.

The person culture is made up of a group of individuals sharing common facilities like an office, equipment or a switchboard. A barristers' chambers or an architectural partnership are good examples.

Handy's final organizational form is the role culture. He names it after Apollo, the god of reason, and represents it as a Greek temple (see Figure 4.2).

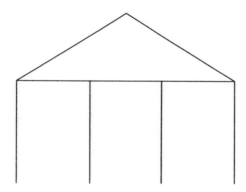

Figure 4.2

Each pillar of the temple consists of a different function. Work in a role culture is controlled by rules and procedures, with each function working independently and co-ordination between them only taking place at the top of the structure, carried out by senior managers.

So how does this relate to the topic of adding value to the benefit of customers, both internal and external? Closely managed and with rapid and responsive decision-making, an effective power culture will focus sharply on the needs of the final or external customer. The language of internal customers is unlikely to be familiar, but the boss will be very aware when quality standards are not being met – and will not be slow to crack the whip in order to bring about improvement.

The task culture is heavily dependent on internal customer relations. Its success depends on team members recognizing and responding to the requirements of other members. The risk is that the task culture will be responsive to the needs of internal customers to the point where the final customer is forgotten.

Members of a person culture, working largely independently, have little need for the techniques of internal customer service, except in so far as they share support staff such as secretaries or administrators.

It is the role culture which runs the greatest risk of a breakdown in customer focus. Controlled, as we have said, through rules and procedures, it is easy to reach a point where 'following the book' becomes more important than satisfying the customer. The means take over from the ends. And, even if the role culture recognizes changes in customer requirements, these can only be addressed by the lengthy process of rewriting the rule book.

Nevertheless, each of these four cultures is relevant to a particular type of organization:

- the power culture to a new, small business, where dynamism and speed of response are critical
- the task culture to an environment of creativity and innovation, where expertise and informality are central to the operation
- the person culture to individuals who work independently, but would benefit from access to common facilities
- the role culture to bureaucratic organizations where it is important to maintain consistency.

The essential operational process must be to ensure that, regardless of the culture of the organization, the voice of the customer is still heard. That is the subject of our next section.

CUSTOMER REQUIREMENTS AND FEEDBACK

Oakland (*Total Quality Management*, Butterworth-Heinemann, 1989) sets out the following questions to be answered in the pursuit of quality:

Customers

- Who are my immediate customers?
- What are their true requirements?
- How do I or can I find out what the requirements are?
- Do I have the necessary capability to meet the requirements? (If not, then what must change to improve the capability?)
- Do I continually meet the requirements? (If not, then what prevents this from happening, when the capability exists?)
- How do I monitor changes in the requirements?

Suppliers

- Who are my immediate suppliers?
- What are my true requirements?
- How do I communicate my requirements?
- Do my suppliers have the capability to measure and meet the requirements?
- How do I inform them of changes in the requirements?

These questions remain relevant, whether customers and suppliers are internal or external.

Researching customer requirements

The use of customer research techniques to identify external customer requirements has been a central part of marketing since the marketing function was first established and formalized. There is a huge variety of techniques, which can be divided into sources of primary and secondary data.

Primary data are facts, figures and opinions collected specifically for a particular purpose. In other words, the data are being collected for the first time. Examples of techniques used to uncover primary data are:

- telephone interviews
- postal surveys
- face-to-face interviews
- focus groups.

Telephone interviews

Telephone interviews are quick. Large numbers of interviews can be conducted in a short space of time. Data can be gathered and processed quickly. They are also cost-effective; costs are considerably less than for face-to-face interviews. Telephone interviews are non-intrusive; a customer may not be willing to spare the time for a face-to-face interview but will spend the time answering questions over the phone.

Telephone interviews do have drawbacks, though. They are sometimes seen as a disguised sales call. People are not usually prepared to spend a long time on a phone interview. Questions need to be kept short and simple. Deep issues – like emotional or psychological responses to products or services – are difficult to extract over the phone. By definition, the sample will be limited to people with a phone! If you want data from business customers, all of whom will have a phone, this does not matter. But if you are researching newspapers, for example, or petfood or window cleaning services, not all your customers will have a phone.

Postal surveys

Postal surveys are sent directly to respondents through the postal system. They offer a quick and relatively inexpensive means of obtaining data. However, the rate of response is often low. (How often have you opened a postal questionnaire and thrown it straight in the bin?) The preparation of the questions is even more critical than with a telephone interview, because there is no one to explain if the meaning of a question is unclear. And, in a world where people read less and watch television more, respondents often lack the patience to complete the survey. As a result, postal surveys often include the offer of an incentive, like entry to a prize draw, if the questionnaire is returned.

Face-to-face interviews

Again involving answers to a set series of questions, face-to-face interviews take place between an individual customer and an interviewer. You may well have been stopped in the street by an interviewer with a clipboard. This will have been part of a quota sampling process, whereby the interviewer is required to interview for example:

- three males under the age of 25
- five women between 30 and 35 with young children
- four businessmen between 35 and 40.

This sample has been constructed to reflect the target population which the product or service being researched is intended to reach.

Alternative approaches to face-to-face interviews involve prebooking the interview, holding it in the respondent's home or office. Face-to-face interviews are costly and time-consuming. However, they allow a more in-depth exploration of issues and give scope for the interviewer to use visual prompts (known as 'flash cards') and to show physical products.

Focus groups

Unlike the other types of survey we have considered, focus groups are reasonably unstructured in the way topics are examined, and the answers are less predictable. These groups depend for their success on a highly skilled and experienced researcher and often take up a whole evening, with drinks and refreshments provided.

> ### CASE STUDY
>
> Prior to the 1997 general election, the New Labour Party recognized the importance of tailoring its policies to the expectations and priorities of the electorate. Although the party was criticized in some quarters for abandoning Old Labour values, it is generally accepted that the use of focus groups made a large contribution to shaping the policies, presentation and image which won the election.

Predictably, focus groups are expensive and time-consuming. Because the discussions may go down an almost infinite variety of routes, the analysis of results is difficult. It is also possible for one strong-minded or opinionated individual to hijack a discussion, unless controlled by the researcher. Nevertheless, focus groups are valuable ways of exploring complex issues, where there is no existing evidence on which to base judgement about what the outcomes may be.

Secondary data is the phrase used to describe information or statistics already collected for a different purpose. Sometimes this will be available in published form. At other times, it may simply be lying around in the organization! Sources of secondary data include:

Internal records

- past sales records
- lost order records
- customer complaints or letters of praise.

Industry data

- trade magazines
- trade association reports
- business school analyses.

Government sources

- Central Statistical Office
- Department of Trade
- Driver and Vehicle Licensing Centre
- Department for Education and Employment
- Customs and Excise
- Inland Revenue
- Office of Population Census and Surveys.

The techniques described so far all provide data and information related to external customers. However, increasingly, organizations are applying similar techniques to assess the quality of their internal customer service.

Of the techniques described, the following are easily transferable to identify internal customer requirements:

- telephone interviews
- postal interviews
- focus groups
- complaints analysis.

Two further techniques apply equally to both customer groups.

Benchmarking

Benchmarking is a way of comparing an organization's performance with other organizations that are regarded as demonstrating best practice. This normally involves subscribing to a benchmarking service which regularly publishes comparative information related to such factors as:

- quality of customer service
- speed of order response
- customer satisfaction.

Whilst benchmarking does not give access to the specific requirements of your specific customers, it does provide guidance on those issues which are important to customer satisfaction and the standards which you should be seeking to achieve.

A simple alternative approach to benchmarking involves an in-house monitoring system which allows different departments or functions to compare performance with others in the organization.

Customer–supplier partnerships

In her book *When Giants Learn to Dance* (Simon and Schuster, 1989) Rosabeth Moss Kanter points out the benefits of closer customer–supplier relationships:

Stakeholder alliances are defined by pre-existing interde-pendence. They are 'complimentary' coalitions between a number of stakeholders in a business process who are involved in different stages of the value-creation chain. Stakeholders are those groups on which an organization depends – the people who can help it achieve its goals or can stop it dead in its tracks. They include suppliers, customers and employees.

Such complimentary alliances tend to be both quality-driven and innovation-driven. Quality for one company's products is often a matter of actions taken by another organization that supplies parts or labour; gaining more control over quality may mean influencing those other organizations. Further, major innovations in technology or organizational systems require longer-term investments. When they also require similar investments from stakeholders, to ensure compatibility of systems, for example, then the basis for an alliance emerges.

Customer–supplier alliances or partnerships, as advocated here, bring a number of advantages:

- They eliminate the traditional adversarial nature of customer–supplier relationships.
- They offer scope for joint product or service development.
- They improve quality.
- They provide suppliers with a deeper understanding of customer requirements.

Kanter's comments concentrate on relations with external suppliers. But her references to employers also raise the question of relations with internal suppliers.

QUESTION

Do you see the relationship with your internal suppliers as co-operative or adversarial?
How often do you meet with them, to make sure that their supplies satisfy your requirements?
To what extent do you help them – and they help you – to improve quality, systems and outputs?

Marks and Spencer (M&S) take a tough line with their suppliers. They demand high quality standards and very competitive prices. But this is not simply a one-way street. M&S will normally send a team of advisers into a new supplier, to recommend ways of improving quality and productivity, and reducing costs and waste. Suppliers who despair of meeting the company's requirements usually find that the advisers' recommendations enable them to improve their output, whilst still making a reasonable profit margin.

Without a doubt, Marks and Spencer have a clear specification for their product requirements. But it is surprising how often a supplier's failure to meet the customer's requirements is because customers don't know exactly what they want – or if they do, fail to make it clear. This is sometimes true of external suppliers – particularly in the context of job or project operations, where the output is unique and the customer has no experience on which to base the specification – but even more so in the case of internal customer–supplier relations. Often this is because the customer takes the internal supplier for granted. The service has always been there and the customer never stops to ask whether it genuinely meets his or her requirements.

QUESTION

Have you ever stopped to ask what you need from your internal supplier?
Even if you have, what have you done to ensure your suppliers understand your requirements?
How well do your internal suppliers understand what you do with the outputs you receive?
Do you communicate the criteria against which you judge their outputs?

REASONABLE AND UNREASONABLE EXPECTATIONS

The customer–supplier relationship is based on a contract. One party provides something, the other receives it and in some way pays for it.

In the case of external relationships, the contract is formal. It is (or should be) based on a formal and detailed specification of requirements, against which the resulting product or service can be assessed for conformance.

CASE STUDY

Most government contracts are let competitively on the basis of an 'invitation to tender' (ITT), issued by the department concerned. The process involved is as follows:

1   The department advertises the forthcoming contract, giving a brief summary of the requirements and inviting 'expressions of interest'.
2   An invitation to tender is sent to all potential contractors who have expressed interest. In the case of a simple requirement, the ITT will run to perhaps fifty pages. In the case of more complex requirements, it may amount to several hundred pages. The ITT specifies the product or service, the criteria against which bids will be assessed, how quality will be assessed and contains details of delivery and how the project will be managed and controlled.
3   Contractor bids will be evaluated for compliance, cost and value for money.
4   The department will choose its preferred contractor.
5   Contractor performance will be monitored against the 'statement of requirements' contained in the original ITT and the resulting contract.
6   Regular review meetings will keep contractors informed about their progress.

There is a powerful logic to this process. Unfortunately, it is rarely applied to internal customer–supplier relationships, which are based on a much more informal and often unspecified contract.

As a result, there is likely to be a wide gulf between customer expectations and supplier delivery. Indeed, if external customer–supplier contracts are not specified with this kind of rigour, a similar gulf may develop.

However, even when customer requirements and expectations are clearly specified and communicated, and performance monitored, it remains fair to ask whether those expectations are reasonable.

Typically, customer requirements will relate to:

■   quality
■   cost
■   speed of delivery
■   volume
■   management of the relationship.

But it is important to recognize that:

- the higher the quality, the greater the cost
- the faster the delivery, the more resources are needed
- the greater the volume, the more it costs and the more resources are needed
- the better the relationship, the more time, effort and expertise are required.

The management literature is currently full of references to quality, excellence, customer service, added value and continuous improvement. All of these have become key objectives for organizations, departments, teams and individuals.

In many cases, their achievement has depended on no more than the elimination of inefficient procedures, wasteful practices, staff incompetence and poor communication. In several organizations, there is still scope to improve in all these areas.

However, we have also pointed out that the process of benchmarking performance sets standards against criteria of best practice. Consequently, all organizations strive to match and outdo the standards achieved by their competitors.

CASE STUDY

The hours worked by British managers have risen steadily since 1979, to the point where they work longer hours than any other managers in Europe. The cost in terms of long-term sickness, early retirement, family breakdown and clinical depression is enormous. The consistent argument in favour of long hours is the need for competitiveness.

In a world where innovation, excellence, quality, service, customer focus, added value and continuous improvement have become the norms or the targets for organizations, the argument based on competitive advantage ceases to apply. In addition, there is a growing recognition that all these attributes cost money.

It is relevant here to quote Charles Dickens's Mr Micawber, who said: '*Income: 20 shillings. Expenditure 20 shillings and 1 penny. Result: Misery.*' In other words, it is essential for both customers and suppliers to recognize the costs involved in improving customer satisfaction, adding value and improving quality. It is reasonable for customers and suppliers to expect these benefits, but not at the expense of the long-term survival of the organization. The processes of improving customer communication and the development of customer–

supplier liaisons or partnerships which we described in this chapter offer the opportunity to ensure that customers can make an informed choice about the standards they are prepared to pay for.

COMPETENCE SELF-ASSESSMENT

1   How would you define your organization's external customers?

2   What are their requirements and expectations?

3   Who are your internal customers?

4   What do they expect from you and how well do you meet their expectations?

5   Does your organization have a customer charter? If so, what real difference does it make to the way people behave?

6   Is your relationship with suppliers co-operative or confrontational?

7   Does your organization have a power, task, person or role culture? Is it suited to the business?

8   If not, what changes would you recommend to improve customer service within it?

9   How do you find out your customers' requirements? What more could you do?

10   Are your customers' expectations reasonable? If not, how could you change their expectations without antagonizing them?

5 Managing quality

Any discussion of quality starts off by facing an immediate problem – the difficulty of defining exactly what we mean by the term. Two quotations from the quality management literature will make this clear:

One of the main difficulties evident in the field of quality management is the variety of terms employed. Many are ill-defined and are used both interchangeably and inconsistently.
(Bell, McBride and Wilson, *Managing Quality*, Butterworth-Heinemann, 1994)

'Is this a quality watch?' Pointing to my wrist I ask a class of students – undergraduates, postgraduates, experienced managers – it matters not. The answers vary:
'No, it's made in Japan'.
'No, it's cheap'.
'No, the face is scratched'.
'How reliable is it?'
'I wouldn't wear it'.
My watch has been insulted all over the world – London, New York, Paris, Sydney, Brussels, Amsterdam, Bradford!

> Very rarely am I told that the quality of the watch depends on what the wearer requires from a watch – a piece of jewellery to give an impression of wealth or a timepiece which gives the required data, including the date, in digital form? Clearly these requirements determine the quality.
> (John S. Oakland, *Total Quality Management*, Butterworth-Heinemann, 1989)

This second quotation provides a basis for the definition of quality which we shall be using throughout this chapter:

> quality describes the extent to which a product or service meets customer requirements.

Two of the leading quality gurus express this idea in different, but similar phrases:

- 'fitness for purpose or use' (Joseph Juran, *Quality Control Handbook*, McGraw-Hill, 1979)
- 'conformance to specification' (Philip Crosby, *Quality is Free*, McGraw-Hill, 1979).

Paradoxically, our definition and the phrases we have quoted offer a warning against assuming that 'quality' is synonymous with 'high quality' or 'Rolls Royce quality'. In some situations, customers may require and specify excellent quality. However, despite the title of Philip Crosby's book, it is important to recognize the essential trade-off between cost and quality standard. Consequently, in other situations customers may expect 'good enough' quality, without being prepared to pay the price for the highest standard.

CASE STUDY

The village of Charlton-on-Otmoor has no street lighting. A committee of villagers was asked by the Highways Department if they wanted it. They refused, preferring to rely on light from local houses rather than pay the extra council tax which street lighting would involve.

Marks and Spencer, Bhs and Littlewoods all offer men's shirts, but of different standards and at different prices. Each range is intended for a different market. If all three retailers offered the same high standard, they would fail to meet the expectations of customers looking for a cheaper product.

Our introduction so far brings together themes from earlier chapters of this book.

IMAGE AND EXPECTATIONS

At a macro level, it is important for operations managers to be aware of:

- the markets which the organization has chosen to serve
- the balance between product or service standard and price or cost which the organization has chosen to offer
- the expectations and requirements of customers in those market segments
- their own contribution to achieving the organization's chosen standards and costs
- their contribution to meeting customer requirements.

At a macro level, or, in different words, at the level of meeting the requirements of internal customers, operations managers need to understand:

- who those internal customers are
- the nature of their needs and expectations
- how much they are prepared to pay to have those needs met
- the customers' views of the trade-off between standard and cost.

In the title to this section we have linked image and expectations. In strategic marketing terms, this linkage is easy to identify.

Oxfam and Scope (formerly the Spastics Society) both operate charity shops. Oxfam has a reputation for higher priced and higher standard second-hand items than Scope. As

> a result, customers go to Oxfam for recent hardback and paperback titles, but to Scope for a cheap holiday read. Similarly, contributors give old items to Scope, new items to Oxfam. In both cases, the image of the organization and the expectations of its customers coincide.

The linkage is more tenuous when it comes to internal markets. However, three considerations should be borne in mind:

- Internal suppliers are increasingly subject to external competition.
- 'Doing without' is a valid option for some internal customers.
- Internal suppliers have an image as much as external customers do.

In consequence, it is important for internal suppliers to assess their image in the internal marketplace and to decide:

- whether that image is consistent with the standard of the product or service offered
- whether the image is consistent with customer expectations
- whether the standard is consistent with the expectations.

Notice that we have stressed 'consistent with'. You will find references in the total quality literature to:

- exceeding customer expectations
- delighting customers.

However, we have also pointed out that quality has a cost. Therefore, it is necessary to evaluate the cost implications of quality improvement, in order to establish whether internal customers are prepared to pay their share of that cost.

THE LANGUAGE OF QUALITY

Three terms recur frequently in discussions about quality. These are:

- quality control
- quality assurance
- total quality management.

The three processes are very different in:

- their objectives
- the operational stage to which they apply
- the systems necessary to support them
- the actions resulting from them.

Let us examine each in turn.

Quality control

Quality control is the traditional process of comparing product or service outputs with customer requirements or specifications. Its purpose is to identify those outputs which do meet, and those which do not meet, the quality specification. Typical systems used in the quality control process are:

- quality inspection, where inspectors assess outputs against specification on a pass/fail or go/no go basis
- output sampling, which reduces the cost of inspection by assessing, say, one in ten of outputs
- statistical process control, which identifies the sources of variance in output quality.

We shall consider these in more detail later in this chapter.

The significant feature of quality control is that it takes place after the event. In other words, it is applied to products and services after they have been finished. This process is easiest to recognize in a manufacturing context, where, for example, finished components are checked for fit or engines are bench-tested when they have been built. However, the quality control process is applied elsewhere as well:

- Proof-reading a letter before it is sent out is a form of quality control.
- Editing a book to ensure the content is accurate is a form of quality control.
- Checking your supermarket bill is a form of quality control, although here it is the customer, rather than the supplier, who does the controlling.

Actions resulting from quality control are either:

- acceptance of outputs which meet the specification, or
- rejection of outputs which do not meet the quality standard.

Quality assurance

Where quality control concentrates on outputs, quality assurance focuses on the various stages of the transformation process. Its objective is therefore to ensure that the methods and procedures which bring about transformation are designed to achieve the required output quality. Thus, while quality control takes place after the event, quality assurance takes place during the event.

Typical quality assurance systems are:

- ISO 9000
- reviews of quality policy
- flow-charting
- design of control documents.

Because quality assurance sets out to prevent quality problems, actions resulting from it are likely to be:

- process redesign
- systems implementation
- streamlining
- clarification of procedures
- allocation of responsibilities
- improved documentation.

Total quality management

Total quality management (TQM) is an all-embracing philosophy which is far wider in its application than the two processes we have considered so far. It is intended to improve the effectiveness and flexibility of businesses as a whole, by organizing and involving the entire organization: every department, every team, every activity, every individual. It is TQM which has given rise to the concept of the internal customer and extended the idea of customer expectations beyond that of output quality alone to include such things as delivery, customer relations, communication and added value.

The TQM philosophy therefore applies before, during and after the event. Support systems will cover a huge range of activities:

- customer consultation and feedback
- training
- process improvement
- systems design
- conformance reviews.

The outcomes of TQM are therefore nothing less than a radical reappraisal of all attitudes, activities and procedures throughout the organization.

It would be dangerous to assume, though, that quality control is less desirable than quality assurance, or that quality assurance is less desirable than total quality management:

- Quality control is largely a local initiative. Output inspection is a fundamental part of operations management.
- Quality assurance, on the other hand, will involve a review of procedures which may well lie outside the scope of operations management alone.
- Total quality management requires the support and involvement of everyone in the organization, from top to bottom and throughout all departments.

So, as you read on, keep two questions in mind:

- Which of these techniques do I have the authority to implement?
- What actions could and should I take to support wider initiatives?

QUALITY CONTROL

All these techniques are designed to detect the incidence of outputs failing to meet specification. In addition, statistical process control seeks to identify the causes of poor quality, as a first step towards eliminating them. It thus forms a halfway house between quality control and quality assurance.

As with any form of performance monitoring, quality control techniques depend on having objective standards against which to measure outputs. As elsewhere, these should be quantified as far as possible, though, when it comes to quality controlling service outputs, it may not always be possible to develop genuinely objective, quantified standards.

Inspection

To be truly effective, quality inspection should take place at each stage of an operation, starting with the first input from an external customer. As we have hinted, writers on quality management are inclined to be dismissive of quality inspection. A quote from Bell, McBride and Wilson (*Managing Quality*, Butterworth-Heinemann, 1994) confirms this point:

There are many systems which can be put into place to minimize the amount of scrap and rework (wrong first time) output from a system. Perhaps the simplest is incoming goods inspection. This is put in place for two key reasons. First, there is an understanding that by letting poor-quality goods enter our system, it is difficult to recover the situation and produce a quality product. Second, we are saying that we do not trust our suppliers and thus our own vendor-rating system. Perhaps the most significant outcome of this scenario is that our organization must perform non-value-added activity in order to achieve an acceptable quality of incoming goods. Through the employment of goods inwards inspectors a very high price is being paid for a product which should have been delivered correctly in the first place.

None the less, quality inspection of incoming goods is an essential fact of life in the real, imperfect world. Consider the consequences of not inspecting incoming goods in the following situations:

- A retail store receives a supplier delivery by lorry. It has travelled a long way. Consider the consequences of the warehouse manager signing for the delivery without checking:
  - whether all the items on the delivery note are really there
  - whether any have been damaged in transit.
- A small training partnership is about to run a training event which starts on Monday at a hotel a hundred miles away. The handouts have just arrived from the local copy shop. Consider the consequences of packing them into the trainer's car without first checking:
  - whether the right number of copies have been taken
  - whether multipage handouts have been collated and stapled in the right order.
- A senior civil servant has been asked to prepare a written answer to a parliamentary enquiry. The answer will be sent to the Member of Parliament who raised the enquiry and a copy placed in the House of Commons library. Consider the consequences if the civil servant does not check that the answer, which has been researched by a subordinate and typed by a secretary, is accurate and relevant in content and contains no grammatical, spelling or typing errors.

In each situation, it is apparent that failure to check input quality runs the risk of leading to:

- overcharging
- disruption or inconvenience
- final customer dissatisfaction
- a loss of face or reputation
- poor output quality.

Even so, it is important to realize that quality control is a costly technique. It requires resources (staff, equipment). It leads to scrap or reworking. It has no possible outcome other than acceptance or rejection. Nevertheless, it is an essential process until such time as every supplier is totally competent and every input and output wholly reliable.

Sampling

Sampling is one way of reducing inspection costs. It is a worthwhile technique where the product or service is complex, making the cost of inspection high, or where the historical rejection rate is low. The quality of samples taken from a batch will lead to a decision as to whether the total batch should be accepted or rejected.

Compared with full inspection, sampling brings the following benefits:

- time saving
- reduced handling damage
- fewer staff required
- more efficient rejection, based on batch rather than individual items.

However, it brings drawbacks too:

- the risk of accepting poor quality batches
- the risk of rejecting good items
- increased likelihood of rejection later in the operation
- less reliable information about inputs and outputs.

To be effective, sampling must be carried out rigorously. In other words, the samples selected for inspection must be chosen according to a sampling method which guarantees that they will be representative and the inspection must be carried out and acceptance/rejection decisions taken with full regard to the seriousness of various defects. The reality of both sampling and inspection is usually rather different:

- Samples are chosen because they are convenient rather than representative.
- Samples are chosen on a regular rather than random basis.
- Outputs which are difficult to access are not sampled.
- Batches are rejected for minor defects.
- Major but infrequent defects slip through.

To overcome these problems, quality sampling requires information on:

- the size of sample which will be statistically reliable
- a way of deriving batch quality from sample quality
- those aspects of quality to be measured and how accept/ reject decisions are taken as a result.

Statistical process control

The technique of statistical process control is based on simple and obvious concepts. However, its implementation involves some complex collection and analysis of data and is therefore likely to require additional resources and senior management support.

Fundamental to operations management is the idea that applying the same transformation process to the same inputs will result in the same outputs – the assumption that the process will remain constant. After all, any batch or continuous operation relies on producing consistent or constant output standards at all times.

Statistical process control starts from the recognition that, in fact, any process, product or service is subject to variation. It also recognizes that such variations stem from two types of causes:

- 'normal' causes which are inherent in the system, possible to reduce but impossible to eliminate and outside the operator's control
- 'special' causes which are unusual factors, resulting in significant variations and which can normally be corrected by the operator.

Examples of normal causes are:

- inconsistencies in raw materials
- unreliable equipment
- inadequately trained staff
- poor product or service design.

Any of these causes will result in variations which will occur according to a normal distribution (traditionally known as a bell-shaped curve), as shown in Figure 5.1.

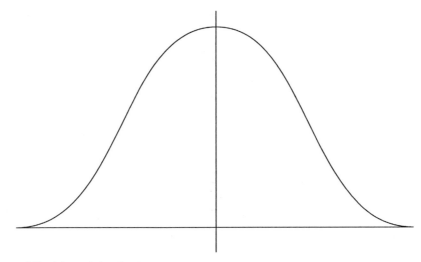

Figure 5.1   Normal distribution

What this means is that variations from the norm will occur in a regular pattern on either side of the mean in Figure 5.1.

Special causes may be:

- equipment breakdown
- faulty adjustment
- operator oversight.

The pattern of special variations will be irregular – some outputs will be adversely affected, others will not.

Statistical process control operates (and this is where the complex analysis comes in) by plotting the pattern of normal variations and superimposing special variations onto them. This process can be applied to individual inputs and to individual quality measures, in such a way as to identify the causes of variation, those which are under the operator's control and those which require management intervention. Thus, as we have said, the technique starts by identifying defects in the form of variations, but moves on to isolate the causes, as a first step to removing them.

RIGHT FIRST TIME

We have adopted this title, rather than the quality assurance phrase we used earlier, because we believe it highlights the key difference between quality control on one hand and quality assurance on the other. Quality control rejects poor quality after it has happened. Quality assurance attempts to ensure that it does not happen at all.

We have already mentioned that the implementation of quality assurance is often associated with the introduction of ISO 9000 or one of its equivalents – ISO 9001, 9002 or 9003. However, it is again necessary to differentiate between theory and practice.

Applied as it was originally intended, the ISO 9000 series provides a methodology with which to establish, document and maintain an effective quality system which will demonstrate to customers an organization's commitment to quality and its ability to meet their quality needs. It expects a critical examination of all of an organization's procedures which have an impact on quality and careful attention to improving and refining them. The process of documentation is intended simply to ensure that best practice, once established, is maintained.

The reality, though, has been different in many cases. Organizations have been content simply to document existing procedures, without taking the essential first step of asking whether they genuinely deliver quality. It is this approach which has given ISO 9000 a bad name!

CASE STUDY

A London-based consultancy with a poor reputation for late delivery and low levels of customer satisfaction nevertheless gained ISO 9001 by carefully documenting its invoicing and consultant booking procedures.

So, what should a quality assurance process look like? Quality assurance involves an analysis of all the processes and procedures in an organization which lead ultimately to the delivery of a product or service to the customer. Each process and procedure is subject to examination, to identify the extent to which it meets the customer's expectations or requirements – the definition of quality that we have used all through this chapter. Traditionally, quality assurance has concentrated on the needs of the final customer. From this viewpoint, all processes and procedures are seen as a single operation – that of creating final customer satisfaction.

Although it would be hard to argue with this philosophy, it has sometimes had the unfortunate result of forcing staff to jump through procedural hoops which, whilst helpful to the final customer, introduce significant inconvenience or disruption to the staff concerned along the way.

CASE STUDY

As described elsewhere in this book, the competitive tendering process used by local and national government is intended to achieve the highest level of value for money for the final customer – the taxpayer. However, along the way, the process will involve:

- national advertising to attract expression of interest
- the publication of an invitation to tender
- briefings for potential suppliers
- an evaluation of bids
- responses to unsuccessful bidders, explaining why they were unsuccessful.

Typically, it will require significant time and staff resources from the originating department, contracts and finance.

The care necessary to make the process error-proof in order to guarantee value for money can mean that the originating department, desperate for its supplies, has to wait six months before the contract is let.

Nowadays, under the influence of total quality management, quality assurance is more likely to view each stage in the creation of final customer satisfaction as a separate operation, each one intended to satisfy the needs of the next internal customer in the value chain.

Quality assurance involves the following steps:

- mapping the operation
- identifying the processes and procedures which support each stage
- assessing each against criteria of customer satisfaction
- highlighting the need for improvement
- monitoring the improvement.

Central to the philosophy of quality assurance is the principle that those responsible for each activity are best placed to evaluate and improve it. However, we have already pointed out the risks of delegated responsibility. Consequently, quality assurance is usually carried out by a network of local project teams, co-ordinated by a central supervising committee or task force.

Mapping the operation/identifying processes

It is the responsibility of the central committee to map the total operation, highlighting the points where handover takes place between functions and isolating individual processes. It is then for local teams to develop more detailed maps of their individual activities.

The more comprehensive these maps, the more useful they will be. As a minimum, they should show the separate steps of a process, the inputs required and the procedures in place.

A simple process flow chart is shown in Figure 5.2 for the production of a wordprocessed report.

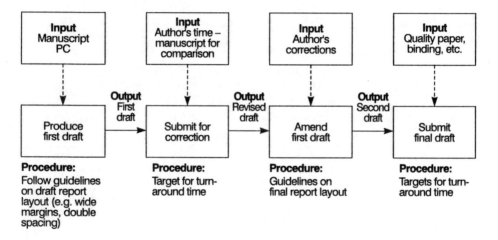

Figure 5.2   Report production process

Assessing/highlighting improvement needs

These stages are central to the process. They should involve both supplier and customer. Their intention is to review critically everything which happens to support each activity and, if necessary, to identify where and why it is failing.

For example, our production of a wordprocessed report requires inputs of an author's manuscript, time, physical stocks of paper and covers. It also depends on the implementation of various procedures and targets. Recognizing that author and wordprocessor (WP) operator are either customer or supplier at different stages of the process, a critical review should ask:

- Is the author's manuscript legible?
- Does the PC have a suitable wordprocessing package?
- Is the author available to make corrections?

- Are the layout guidelines up to date and easy to understand?
- Are the turnaround targets realistic, in view of the WP operator's workload and the author's availability?
- If not, what should change?
- Are suitable covers and paper readily available?

Potential improvement needs from this analysis might include:

- a more user-friendly WP package
- layout guidelines to be rewritten
- faster access to author for corrections
- paper stocks to be held closer to the WP operator's desk.

Implementing and monitoring improvement

It is unusual for quality assurance methods to be introduced for a single process. Usually, they will be applied across an organization, or at least to a whole department. The responsibility for the implementation of improvement is therefore likely to be spread.

This is where the central committee has a further task to do. Having mapped the overall operation, allocated individual activities for review and supervised that work against agreed deadlines, it is important for them now to co-ordinate the outcomes. For example, some outdated or inaccurate procedures, like our report layout guidelines, may emerge as improvement needs across the organization. Others, like the maintenance or ordering of stationery stock, may require company-wide or local action.

Yet other improvement needs – like faster or easier access to the author for corrections – will need to be implemented through negotiation between the parties concerned.

Overall, though, the quality assurance process is designed to result in action which will eliminate or correct any factors which prejudice the achievement of customer satisfaction, both at the end of the value chain and at any stage along it.

As we pointed out at the beginning of the section, quality assurance introduces systems which ensure, as far as possible, that products and services are 'right first time'. It may therefore seem illogical to suggest that those systems, once introduced, need monitoring. However, all systems are subject to neglect, corruption and abuse.

Monitoring should focus on three areas:

- current suitability
- systems maintenance
- output monitoring.

Current suitability

This is to do with the extent to which systems are still relevant to the organization's current operating environment. It is quite likely that, over time, the goals and objectives of the organization have changed, improved technology has become available or operational outputs are needed sooner or quicker. Faced with any of these factors, it will be necessary to review, update or upgrade the systems – and that can only be done if the divergence between the environment and the system has been recognized.

Systems maintenance

Over time, systems and processes degrade and become less efficient. As a result of ignorance, laziness or attempts to keep a sagging system in operation, it will be changed, simplified or made more complex. The first stage of systems maintenance is, as just described, to assess its current suitability. If it is found still to be suitable, the next stage is to establish whether it is being used as originally designed.

If not, this may show up a need for:

- staff training
- a change in attitude
- an evaluation of the match between the needs of the system and available resources
- an assessment of the costs and benefits of the outputs from the system.

Output monitoring

Quite simply, this is a question of establishing whether outputs continue to create quality by meeting customer needs. The needs may have changed, or the quality of the output may have declined. In either case, this highlights a need to go back into the quality assurance cycle once more.

QUALITY IMPROVEMENT

We have chosen this title for our final section because it is a fair reflection of the central theme of total quality management, our last and most ambitious approach to quality management.

As you will have gathered, TQM is a philosophy which puts customer satisfaction at the heart of the organization. Put in those terms, it may not sound particularly revolutionary. After all, for many years organizations, particularly trading companies, have operated with slogans like:

- 'The customer is king.'
- 'The customer is always right.'
- 'The customer is our only reason for existence.'

In most of us, though, the cynic (or the realist!) recognizes that, whilst such slogans were relevant to – and to a greater or lesser extent accepted by – customer-facing staff like members of the sales force or retail shop assistants, their application did not go much further.

With hindsight, as we explored in Chapter 4, it is obvious that:

- hospitals have customers
- schools have customers
- churches have customers
- charities have customers
- government departments have customers.

Nevertheless, it is only since the late 1970s that this point has been recognized. And that recognition of colleagues and other departments as internal customers is a process which many organizations are still struggling with.

CASE STUDY

A government department, as part of its competence-based training initiative, decided to introduce a package on TQM. The consultants hired to write the package found, to their consternation, that neither the trainers working there, nor the Training Manager involved, could understand the idea of 'internal customers'. The resulting package had more to do with quality control and quality assurance than it did with TQM!

The implementation of a TQM philosophy demands:

- commitment and support from all levels of management, starting at the top. This theme was developed, along with other issues, in Chapter 2.
- A culture which encourages customer focus, experimentation and improvement. This theme was introduced in Chapter 4 and is expanded further in Chapters 8 and 9.
- managers who are adept at managing people. This is the main thrust of Chapter 10.

- a view of the organization as a total system, made up of activities designed to create customer satisfaction. This theme was explored earlier in this chapter.
- a practical, empowering approach to managing people. This is a recurrent theme of this book, particularly in Chapters 3, 6, 8, 9 and 10.

You will recognize from this that the TQM philosophy has had a major impact on the approaches, techniques, processes and attitudes which now underpin operations management. However, when you remember that we defined the purpose of operations as being to provide a service to the customer or client, this will come as no surprise!

COMPETENCE SELF-ASSESSMENT

1   How does your organization define quality? Would you agree with that definition?

2   What image do your customers have of your operation? Is it consistent with:
    (a) the standard you deliver?
    (b) their requirements?

3   How could you use the following quality control methods to improve quality in your operation:
    (a) inspection?
    (b) sampling?
    (c) statistical process control?

4   How could you use the following quality assurance techniques to improve quality in your operation:
    (a) operation mapping?
    (b) evaluating processes and procedures?
    (c) highlighting improvement needs?
    (d) monitoring systems?

5   What management support would you need to implement your chosen methods?

6   What benefits would you highlight to gain the support?

7   How customer-focused is:
    (a) your organization?
    (b) your operation?

8   Does your organization have a culture which would support TQM?

9   If not, what would have to change?

10 How much of TQM philosophy can you implement personally?

6 Health, safety – and productivity?

In 1997, the British Health and Safety Executive, which is responsible for advising on health and safety issues and for administering health and safety law, took as its slogan the motto: Good health is good business.

At first reading, that may not appear to make sense. After all, surely good business depends on:

- keeping costs down
- maintaining cost-efficient output
- avoiding labour disputes
- producing what customers want to buy?

So, what do all those have to do with maintaining effective health and safety policies and procedures? Surprisingly, a great deal. As we shall explain in this chapter, a considerable body of criminal and civil law means that failure to provide a safe and healthy working environment for staff is likely to result in expensive and time-consuming court appearances. Health and safety legislation places significant responsibilities on employers and employees. And, as with other legislation, ignorance of the law is no excuse. Further, a poor health and safety record is likely to bring with it difficulties in recruiting and retaining staff, major losses in productivity and, in cases where external customers have adopted a partnership relationship with suppliers as we described in Chapter 4, the risk of losing potentially profitable contracts.

In order to reflect these issues, this chapter presents four key themes:

- the legal framework of health and safety
- management and individual rights and responsibilities
- the price of failure
- the link to productivity.

Each of these themes is the subject of a different section.

THE LEGAL FRAMEWORK

Most readers of this book are likely to associate health and safety legislation with the Health and Safety at Work etc. Act, 1974. Whilst this is certainly the most influential and far-reaching piece of legislation, it was not the first and is definitely not the only one which has an impact on health and safety issues and procedures in an organization.

Other relevant legislation passed before 1974 includes:

- The Factories Act, 1937
- The Factories Act, 1967
- The Offices, Shops and Railway Premises Act, 1963
- The Factories (Cleanliness of Walls and Ceilings) Regulations, 1960
- The Fire Precautions Act, 1971.

Although most of the provisions of these Acts and regulations have been incorporated into later legislation, some still apply.

Legislation brought in after 1974, mainly intended to clarify some of the general obligations contained in the 1974 Act, includes:

- The Reporting of Injuries, Diseases and Dangerous Occurrences Regulations, 1985
- The Health and Safety (First Aid) Regulations, 1981
- The Safety Representatives and Safety Committees Regulations, 1977
- The Noise at Work Regulations, 1989
- The Electricity at Work Regulations, 1989
- The Provision and Use of Work Equipment Regulations, 1992
- The Manual Handling Operations Regulations, 1992
- The Health and Safety (Display Screen Equipment) Regulations, 1992

- The Control of Substances Hazardous to Health Regulations, 1994
- The Personal Protective Equipment at Work Regulations, 1992
- The Workplace (Health, Safety and Welfare) Regulations, 1992
- The Management of Health and Safety at Work Regulations, 1992.

It is unlikely that, as an operations manager, you will need to be able to quote chapter and verse from all of these. However, the Health and Safety at Work Act, 1974, and the Management of Health and Safety at Work Regulations, 1992, both place considerable obligations on all managers, as we shall see later. Consequently, it is essential that you know and understand those two pieces of legislation. That is the purpose of this section, although we shall refer to some of the other legislation at times, where this gives a more useful or more detailed explanation of the other two pieces.

The Health and Safety at Work Act, 1974

This Act was deliberately drafted to make health and safety central issues for all organizations, regardless of their size, ownership or the nature of their operations, and to make health and safety the responsibility not only of the organization itself, but also of manufacturers, suppliers and staff.

The Act does this by imposing general 'duties of care' on various groups of people. We can summarize these duties as follows.

Employers' duties

Employers are under a general duty to ensure, so far as is reasonably practicable, the health and safety and welfare at work of all their employees. This includes:

- the provision and maintenance of plant and systems of work that are safe and without risks to health
- arrangements for ensuring safety and absence of risks to health in connection with the use, handling, storage and transport of articles and substances
- the provision of such information, instruction, training and supervision as is necessary to ensure the health and safety at work of their employees
- the maintenance of any place of work under their control in a condition that is safe and without risks to health, and the provision and maintenance of means of access to and from the place of work that are safe and without such risks

■ the provision and maintenance of a working environment for employees which is safe, without risks to health and with adequate regard to facilities and arrangements for their welfare at work.

Employees' duties

All employees are under a duty to take reasonable care for the health and safety at work of themselves and any other people who might be affected by their acts or omissions, and to co-operate with their employers and others to enable them to comply with statutory duties and requirements. Additionally, they must not intentionally or recklessly misuse anything provided in the interests of health, safety or welfare in pursuance of any aspect of health and safety law.

Manufacturers', designers', importers' and suppliers' duties

People in these categories have a duty to:

■ ensure, so far as is reasonably practicable, that articles are designed and constructed in such a manner as to be safe and without risks to health when being set, used, cleaned, maintained or stored in 'reasonably foreseeable circumstances'
■ ensure, so far as is reasonably practicable, that substances are safe and without risks to health when being used, handled, processed, stored or transported
■ ensure that necessary tests and examinations are carried out
■ provide adequate information about the uses, tests and any conditions which must be observed in the use of articles or substances.

We shall examine what these duties involve in practical terms a little later in this chapter. At this stage, though, it is worth highlighting how frequently the phrase 'as far as is reasonably practicable' occurs. In broad terms, this involves balancing the degree of risk to employees against the money, time or effort required to minimize the risk.

However, it would be a mistake to treat the phrase as an escape clause. Traditionally, the courts, even before the passing of the 1974 Act, have taken a hard line on employers' responsibilities, as the following case illustrates.

CASE STUDY

Smith v. Chesterfield and District Co-operative Society Ltd (1953)

The plaintiff, Smith, worked a rolling machine which rolled puff pastry. The machine was fitted with a guard to prevent the operator from having access to the rollers, though there was a three-inch gap at the bottom of the guard. On one occasion, the plaintiff, acting contrary to instructions, pushed her hand under the guard to press some dough back into the machine and was injured when her fingers came into contact with the rollers.

The Court of Appeal decided that the conduct of the plaintiff, unreasonable though it was, was reasonably foreseeable by the defendants. Since the guard provided was such that the plaintiff could put her hand beneath it and thus come into contact with the rollers, the rollers of the machine were not securely fenced within the meaning of the Factories Act, 1937. Therefore the defendants were in breach of their duty under the Act.

The Management of Health and Safety at Work Regulations, 1992

These regulations impose a duty on all employers to assess what health and safety risks their employees, visitors, the self-employed or employees of another organization working on the site may be exposed to as a result of their work. Having made the assessment, the employer must decide what steps will be taken to protect those concerned, in accordance with relevant health and safety legislation. Where five or more workers are employed, the employers must keep a record of:

- the findings of the risk assessment
- the actions taken to reduce or remove the risk identified.

In addition, the regulations make employers responsible for:

- appointing one or more 'competent' persons to help them identify risks and find solutions. These will be people with enough training and experience to enable them to assist the employer properly in a particular area
- carrying out health surveillance and keeping health records for each individual if the work situation brings a risk of particular health problems or diseases developing

- setting up procedures to be followed in the event of serious and imminent danger and nominating enough 'competent' people to implement those procedures if the need arises
- informing employees about any health and safety risks which have been identified and the actions being taken to protect them
- providing adequate and suitable health and safety training.

Finally, the regulations also spell out the duty on employees to follow health and safety instructions, and to report to the employer any dangerous situations in the workplace or any shortcomings in health and safety arrangements.

RIGHTS AND RESPONSIBILITIES

Employers' rights and responsibilities

Employers' rights with respect to health and safety are reasonably self-evident from the summaries of the legislation we have already given. They are entitled to expect that anyone who supplies them with items of equipment or substances for use in the workplace, or who erects or installs equipment, will:

- ensure, so far as is reasonably practicable, that the equipment supplied is so designed and constructed as to be safe and without risks to health when properly used or, in the case of a substance, is safe and without risk to health when properly used
- carry out or arrange for the carrying out of such testing and examination as may be necessary for the supply of equipment and substances which are safe and without risk to health when properly used
- take such steps as may be necessary to make sure that adequate information is available about the use for which equipment or substances have been designed, made and tested, and about any conditions necessary to ensure that, when the equipment or substance is put to that use, it will be safe and without risk to health
- in the case of erecting or installing equipment for use at work in any premises, ensure, as far as is reasonably practicable, that nothing about the way it is erected or installed makes it unsafe or a risk to health when properly used.

Employers also have the right to expect that their employees will:

- take reasonable care for the health and safety of themselves and of other persons who may be affected by their acts or omissions at work
- co-operate as far as is necessary with their employers to enable duties and requirements imposed by the relevant Acts and regulations to be carried out or complied with
- avoid reckless or intentional interference with or misuse of anything provided in the interests of health, safety or welfare
- follow health and safety instructions
- report any dangerous situations in the workplace or shortcomings in health and safety arrangements.

Employers' responsibilities will take rather longer to explain. The practical actions required by the various duties imposed on an employer include:

- the preparation of a written statement of health and safety policy, if the employer has five or more members of staff. Moreover, the policy must be brought to the attention of every employee and a copy given to contractors or other people who work on the company's premises, either regularly or for long periods. It must include a general statement of policy concerning health and safety, the arrangements in place for implementing the policy, details of any specific hazards and the rules designed to deal with them.

    An example of a health and safety policy statement is shown below.

The Directors recognize their responsibility, insofar as it lies within their power, for ensuring health, safety and welfare at work of all employees and visitors. To this end it will be the company's policy to promote and give high priority to the maintenance of a healthy and safe working environment. We seek the co-operation of all employees for that purpose.

All working conditions will comply with the relevant statutory requirements and officially approved codes of practice that are designed to ensure high standards of health and safety.

Particular attention will be paid to:

- providing safe and healthy premises with adequate amenities maintaining plant, machinery and equipment in a safe condition
- providing information, instruction and supervision to enable all employees to contribute positively to their own health and safety at work
- making safe arrangements for the storage, handling and movement of materials and substances
- ensuring that systems of work are safe and healthy
- providing adequate facilities and arrangements for welfare at work.

The company expects its employees on their part to recognize that they have a duty to take every reasonable precaution to avoid harm to themselves, their colleagues and visitors.

Signed:
(Chief Executive)

Date:

- consulting with safety representatives or a safety committee appointed by a recognized trade union (a 'recognized' trade union in this context is one with which the employer bargains over matters such as pay and conditions, disciplinary processes or termination of employment).

    The position of a safety representative or membership of a safety committee confers significant rights on individual employees, which we shall examine later in this section.
- informing employees about health and safety. Employers are required to bring to the attention of their employees certain information about health and safety law and to provide them with the local addresses of the authorities which enforce that law. In order to do this, they may either display an approved poster in the workplace or supply their employees with an approved leaflet. Posters and leaflets are both produced by the Health and Safety Executive and are available from Her Majesty's Stationery Office.

Leaflets, when used, must be given to every employee, together with the local addresses of the relevant enforcing authority, which may be the Health and Safety Executive in the case of factories, farms or building sites, or the local authority in the case of offices, shops, hotels and catering establishments and leisure activities. They must also be given local addresses of the Health and Safety Executive's Employment Medical Advisory Service. Posters must be readily accessible and visible and kept in a good, readable condition. The addresses of the enforcing authority and the Employment Medical Advisory Service must be displayed on the poster.

- reporting all fatal accidents and cases of major injury (for example, fractures of the skull, spine, arm or leg, amputations, loss of sight, electric shock leading to loss of consciousness) by the quickest available means.

- keeping records of reportable injuries for at least three years. Records must include date and time of the accident, where it happened, name and occupation of the injured person, the nature of the injury and how it happened.

- making adequate first-aid provision for employees. The Health and Safety (First Aid) Regulations, 1981 leave it up to the employer to decide what is adequate, taking into account such factors as the number of employees, the nature of the work, the location of the worksite and distance from medical services. As a minimum, though, every employer must keep at least one first-aid box, appoint at least one trained first aider and display at least one notice giving the location of first-aid equipment and the names and locations of first aiders.

In addition, employers have all the responsibilities set out in the Workplace (Health, Safety and Welfare) Regulations, 1992, which relate to:

- temperature
- ventilation
- lighting
- room size
- workstations and seating
- floors and traffic routes
- windows and ventilators
- doors and gates
- escalators
- toilets
- washing facilities

- drinking water
- rest rooms
- facilities for changing and storing clothes.

Employers are also subject to the general duties of care related to the provision and maintenance of plant and systems of work; the use, handling, storage and transport of articles and substances; information, training, instruction and supervision; the maintenance of sites and premises; the provision and maintenance of safe ways into and out of places of work; and of a safe and healthy working environment, to which we have already referred.

The practical implementation of these duties is likely to require, for example:

- regular testing and maintenance of equipment
- the provision of adequate trolleys for moving goods
- dealing with slippery floors, worn carpets or poor drainage
- external lighting
- clearly marked emergency exits
- attention to health and safety during induction training
- extractor fans to remove dust
- protective guards and shields round machinery
- regular checks for obstructions, loose cables, ill-fitting doors or windows.

Individuals' rights and responsibilities

It is obvious from what we have said so far that individual members of staff have the right to a workplace which is safe, healthy and makes adequate provision for their welfare. In more detail, that includes such things as:

- a workplace temperature of at least 16°C, except where work is strenuous and involves physical effort, when a temperature of 13°C is considered reasonable
- sufficient and suitable lighting, without glare
- fresh air
- the removal of harmful dust and fumes
- rest rooms and rest areas which protect non-smokers from discomfort caused by tobacco smoke
- suitable rest facilities for pregnant women and those who are breast feeding
- suitable and sufficient facilities for eating meals
- hot drinks facilities

- access to hot meals, or the means for employees to heat their own food
- the provision of personal protective equipment (such as safety helmets, goggles, gloves, boots, protective clothing), without charge
- suitable workstations, equipment, workbreaks, eye tests and training for users of visual display units (VDUs) and other display screen equipment
- suitable and safe electrical equipment and systems
- personal ear protection where noise levels exceed 85d(A)
- to be briefed on procedures to be followed in case of fire
- access to adequate fire-fighting equipment
- a workplace and equipment which are in efficient working order and good repair.

These rights are drawn from a cross-section of the regulations we mentioned earlier in this chapter and are the entitlement of every employee, regardless of their job, or the size or nature of the organization that employs them.

There are some special rights, in addition, for members of staff who are appointed as safety representatives or members of a safety committee. Such staff are entitled to:

- be consulted about the introduction of any measures in the workplace substantially affecting the health and safety of employees
- be consulted about the appointment of 'competent' persons to identify and solve health and safety risks
- be consulted about health and safety training
- investigate employee complaints about health, safety or welfare
- make representations to the employer about matters affecting health, safety and welfare at work
- carry out inspections of the workplace
- represent employees in consultation with inspectors from enforcing authorities
- receive information from inspectors on matters concerning health, safety and welfare
- paid time to carry out these duties
- access to information and documentation kept under safety legislation (for example, accident records)
- inspect workplace areas at least every three months.

As far as responsibilities are concerned, we have already explored individual obligations to co-operate, not to interfere, to follow instructions and to report dangers or shortcomings. These apply to all employees, regardless of job, grade or level in the organization.

In a management text, though, it is worth spending some time exploring the manager's responsibilities. From the viewpoint of health and safety legislation, managers are in the uncomfortable position of needing to fulfil both employers' and employees' responsibilities. As representatives of their employer, managers are responsible for contributing to the provision and maintenance of a healthy and safe workplace. As members of the workforce, they are at the same time responsible for reporting dangers and shortcomings.

In the first position, they will be involved in:

- monitoring the extent to which the work environment for which they are responsible conforms to the provisions of health and safety legislation
- identifying and taking local remedial action
- ensuring their own awareness and understanding of their organization's health and safety policy and procedures
- briefing and training their staff in that policy and those procedures.

In the second position, they will be a key source of information about dangers and shortcomings which are inherent in the organization's approach to health and safety and which are not susceptible to local correction.

But a manager's responsibilities are wider than those resulting from health and safety legislation. An effective manager should:

- deal humanely and appropriately with injured employees. This will involve giving them comfort and support, taking them if possible to somewhere private to await medical attention, perhaps accompanying them to hospital and notifying the next of kin.
- manage the rest of the department or section. This will mean: getting people back to work, not so much for reasons of productivity but more to lessen shock by restoring a normal routine; arranging time, space and counselling for anyone who is too shocked to continue working.
- learn from the incident. This will involve: identifying the causes of the accident or injury and taking action to ensure that continued working will not lead to its repetition; recording the incident and drawing any necessary conclusions about the prevention of similar events in the future.
- take account of safety considerations when planning the process or output volume of an operation.

- check the safety status of all operations or activities under their control on a regular basis, perhaps by using a safety checklist.
- monitor the provision and use of safety equipment and devices on all activities performed under their supervision.
- encourage their staff to report unsafe processes or conditions and either take corrective action or involve others in doing so.
- maintain a dialogue with the organization's safety specialist in order to ensure that practices and procedures remain safe.

THE PRICE OF FAILURE

In this section, we shall examine separate costs which between them make up the price of failure to deliver and implement effective health and safety practices:

- the legal costs
- the improvement costs
- the output costs.

The legal costs

It should be remembered that the Health and Safety at Work Act, 1974 is a piece of criminal legislation. In other words, breaches of the Act are a criminal offence and action to deal with them will be taken by the state.

This gives rise to our first legal cost. An employer found guilty of failure to carry out any of the various duties of care imposed by the Act will be liable to:

- imprisonment of up to two years
- an unlimited fine.

But that is only the start. Managers who fail to implement policies and procedures set up by their employers are also liable under the Act. And, finally, employees who fail to carry out their own health and safety responsibilities as defined by the Act are also legally liable.

Not surprisingly, this principle of 'joint and several responsibility' makes the health and safety legislation complicated to enforce, because of the need to establish who was at fault when a breach took place. For example, in a manufacturing environment, an employee on piece-rate may deliberately choose to ignore safety instructions because adherence to them will reduce his output. In such a case, the court will need to decide:

- whether the employer made reasonable efforts to ensure that the employee understood and was trained in the relevant safe practices
- whether the employee's manager or supervisor made a conscious decision to overlook the employee's failure to follow safe practices
- whether those practices gave scope for the employee to ignore or get round them.

But those are only the costs arising from criminal law. There are others resulting from civil law.

The 1974 Act states that failure to comply with any of the duties set out in the Act shall not be taken to confer a right of action in civil proceedings. Consequently, the Act creates no new civil liability.

However, the ordinary action for negligence at common law remains available. In cases where, for example, an employee has been injured as a result of the employer's failure to carry out duties under the Act, the employee will need to prove such failure in order to win civil damages. If the employer has already been convicted under civil law, the employee's claim is almost certain to succeed.

The improvement costs

So far, we have said nothing about the work of health and safety inspectors. Health and safety inspectors, employed by either the Health and Safety Executive or local authorities, depending on industry, are entitled to:

- enter any premises at any reasonable time (or at any time if they believe a situation to be dangerous)
- require a police officer, or anyone else authorized by the enforcing authority, to accompany them if they believe they are likely to be obstructed
- bring with them any equipment or materials
- inspect the premises
- carry out any investigation or examination they consider necessary, including taking measurements, photographs or any other kind of recording
- order that the premises be left undisturbed while they carry out the investigation
- take samples of anything found on the premises, or have it dismantled or tested

- demand to be shown any book or document they consider necessary, not just those which have to be kept by law
- require the use of facilities (such as an office) or obtain any help and assistance they feel they might need
- interview and ask questions of anyone they consider appropriate, either alone or in the presence of any witness or other person whom the inspector has invited or allowed to be present. The person interviewed may then be required to sign a declaration of the truth of his or her answers.

In addition, inspectors are also granted any other power necessary for them to enforce the law. It is obvious from this that any organization with a poor safety record or reputation is likely to suffer significant costs arising from the disruption of an inspector's visits. However, the costs go further, because inspectors also have the right to serve improvement and prohibition notices.

Under the 1974 Act, an inspector who is of the opinion that a person is contravening one or more of the statutory provisions relating to health and safety, or has done so in the past and is likely to do so again, is entitled to serve an improvement notice requiring the person concerned to put matters right within the period specified in the notice.

Further, if an inspector is of the opinion that activities as they are carried on, or about to be carried on, involve a risk of serious personal injury, the inspector is entitled to serve a prohibition notice on the person controlling those activities, giving the inspector's reasons for considering them unsafe but, more importantly from a cost viewpoint, requiring them to cease immediately.

The output costs

The previous paragraph in fact explains the first of our output costs. In simple terms, health and safety legislation gives inspectors the right to shut down any activity they consider to be seriously unsafe – with obvious implications for output. But there are other output costs:

- the cost of time off work for sick or injured employees
- the cost of damaged or lost production
- the potential costs of damaged equipment
- the costs of rectification.

Failure to take health and safety seriously is an expensive business! So ask yourself:

- Am I familiar with the health and safety practices and procedures which my employer has laid down relevant to my staff?

- Do I enforce or ignore them?
- Do I support health and safety training, or treat it as unimportant?
- How much attention do I pay to my operation's health and safety record?
- Am I overlooking any trends or particular hazards?
- How much output do I lose as a result of poor health and safety?

Your answers to those questions may well cause some discomfort!

THE LINK TO PRODUCTIVITY

The emphasis of this chapter so far has been on legal, practical and financial considerations. In this final section, we shall examine the impact of health and safety on people issues and the consequences for productivity. We can separate the issues into two categories:

- individual reactions
- union reactions.

Individual reactions

CASE STUDY

Picture two businesses in similar industries. One has a poor health and safety reputation, the other has a better one. The business with the poor reputation pays more than the other. Which, in your opinion, will find it easier to attract staff?

There is no absolutely right answer to that question. It will depend on, amongst other things:

- the unemployment rate in the area
- the wider reputation of both businesses
- the sophistication of the local workforce
- how stable or profitable each business is perceived to be.

Nevertheless, we do believe that there is a link between health and safety on the one hand and ease of recruiting staff on the other. To start with, as was explained earlier in this chapter, an organization which pays attention to health and safety is conveying a more general message about the way it looks after its people. That message is that the organization cares for its staff. A willingness to provide comfortable rest areas, effective training, to evaluate and minimize risks and, overall, to treat staff as valuable resources, has wider implications in terms of making the organization 'a business where people matter'.

Such a reputation in the community may not be enough to compensate for uncompetitively low wage rates. Nevertheless, as any management textbook will tell you, the combination of adequate salaries, rewarding work and a comfortable work environment will do more to attract and retain staff than a big salary alone. It is also worth remembering that the current economic climate allows little scope for organizations to pay staff over the odds. So, since careful attention to staff health, safety and welfare is a legal requirement, it would seem perverse to incur costs by breaching the law – and have to pay staff extra for the privilege! Then how does health and safety impact on an organization's actual workforce? Of course, productivity falls when an employee is injured. But it goes further than that. In organizations where ill-health, accidents and injuries are commonplace:

- Employers lose the confidence of the workforce.
- Managers lose the confidence of the workforce.
- Staff are more concerned about their own well-being than they are about that of the business.

Equally, where the organization and its managers are careful about health, safety and welfare issues, the opposite applies. It is also important to recognize the effect on colleagues of an injury or accident to a member of staff. Other employees working next to the victim, or who are on close personal terms with the victim, may need:

- treating for shock
- time off work to recover
- transporting home.

Union issues

In the 1990s the relationship between employers and unions has, in many organizations, changed from one of confrontation to one of co-operation. It is frequent nowadays to see unions and management working together to improve productivity and efficiency, cut costs, develop more successful working practices and, thereby, to make the organization more effective and see off the competition.

Nevertheless, as is the case with individual employees, such a constructive relationship between employers and unions is dependent on a high degree of trust and a common purpose. Unions, rightly, see their primary responsibility being to safeguard their members. An important part of that responsibility is to look after their members' health, safety and welfare. Consequently, employers who choose to ignore their duties under health and safety legislation will find it difficult or impossible to establish common cause with recognized unions in the workplace.

We have already referred to a recognized union's right to nominate safety representatives, and the right of those representatives to request the formation of a safety committee. The latter is likely to be made up of:

- union representatives
- management representatives
- ex-officio members, possibly in the form of technical specialists.

Those rights are only legally supported in organizations which recognize a trade union. However, there is nothing to stop a non-union organization from seeking safety representatives from its workforce, nor from forming a safety committee.

In a unionized workplace, it is important to recognize the contribution which a safety committee can potentially make. With union–management relationships increasingly taking on the nature of joint problem-solving, a safety committee must, to achieve its potential, be seen as a problem-solving forum. It should not be seen as a forum for bargaining or negotiation, but rather as somewhere for all those involved to seek the best ways in which the employer can ensure that employees' health and safety is safeguarded.

COMPETENCE SELF-ASSESSMENT

1   What is the standard of the health and safety training your organization provides? How could it be improved?

2   What do you do to ensure that your staff understand their health and safety obligations? What more could you do?

3   How often do you carry out a health and safety check of your operation? Is it often enough?

4   What are the principal hazards in your work area? How could these be reduced?

5   What patterns are apparent from the accident records for your area? What could be done about them?

6   What does your organization's health and safety policy say? How do you implement it practically?

7   What are the first aid provisions in your area? Are they adequate?

8   What health and safety improvements could be made to your team's work environment (for example, machine guards, fencing, lighting, ventilation, seating, floors, obstacles)?
9   How satisfactory are the safety practices and procedures relevant to you and your team? How could they be improved?
10   What health and safety records are kept in your organization and who keeps them?

7 Monitoring and control

'Ah now', said our accountant. 'This chapter is where I should really come into my own. Monitoring – that's all to do with checking up on people. And nobody does that better than we do. Accounting techniques offer an ideal way of measuring performance – they reduce everything to standard money values, so it's easy to make comparisons. Budgets and budgetary control are essential to any monitoring system.'

'Well, I'm sorry to disagree with you yet again', replied our personnel officer. 'But for a lot of the time financial performance is too far removed from what people do on a day-to-day basis. Of course, there are exceptional cases. A salesperson, for example, spends his time winning orders, so it would be reasonable to judge his performance on the basis of their monetary value. But even that wouldn't show the whole picture. Order value doesn't tell you much about how well he manages his time, or the quality of his visit reports, or even whether his customers like him. And how could you use financial information to monitor the effectiveness of a nurse's work, or a teacher's, or a road-sweeper's? I suppose you might measure the cost of the swabs a nurse uses, or how much chalk the teacher gets through – but those would hardly reflect the essential nature of the work they do.'

It should come as no surprise that, as in previous chapters, some of these comments are helpful and accurate, whilst others are definitely misleading. But, in order to be able to separate the two, it will be helpful if we start by defining what is meant by the monitoring and control process.

THE MANAGER'S ROLE

Since Henri Fayol published the first book on management theory (*Administration Industrielle et Générale*, 1916), management authors have made repeated attempts to define what a manager does. There are, naturally, differences in their views and emphases. However, there is general agreement amongst most authors of the so-called 'classical' school of management that a manager is responsible for:

- planning
- organizing
- directing or motivating
- controlling.

Managers plan by setting objectives, forecasting, analysing problems and making decisions. They organize by deciding on what activities are necessary to achieve the objectives, classifying the work and allocating it to groups and individuals. They direct or motivate (different authors use both these words to mean the same thing) by communicating to and inspiring their staff. And, finally, they control by checking performance against plans.

These four functions or activities of management are fundamental to the monitoring and control process. They emphasize that a manager controls by measuring or comparing performance against predetermined objectives or plans. The final stage is then to identify differences between planned and actual performance, and to take remedial action to correct them.

We can therefore say that:

- monitoring involves measuring performance against expectations
- control involves taking action to correct discrepancies.

How then should we respond to our accountant's comments? From the preceding definitions, it is obviously correct to say that monitoring performance involves measurement and comparison. It is also true that it is a checking process. But monitoring should not be seen simply as checking up on people. All aspects of operations are susceptible to monitoring – systems, procedures, processes, as well as the performance of people. It is also a mistake to attempt to base monitoring exclusively on financial indicators and comparisons. In some cases these are relevant, but in others, as our personnel officer points out, there are more helpful and meaningful indicators against which to measure performance.

OBJECTIVES AND PERFORMANCE MEASURES

In Chapter 2 of this book, we described a 'top-down, bottom-up' approach to strategic planning which started with senior management defining an organization's mission and goals, then involving staff lower down the organization in formulating their own objectives and plans in order to contribute to them.

Consequently, it is essential that individual objectives and performance standards should all be couched in such a way as to contribute to the success of the overall organization. As Peter Drucker remarks (in his book *The Practice of Management*, Butterworth-Heinemann, 1968):

> Each member of the enterprise contributes something different, but they must all contribute towards a common goal. Their efforts must all pull in the same direction and their contributions must fit together to produce a whole – without gaps, without friction, without unnecessary duplication of effort.
>
> Business performance therefore requires that each job be directed towards the objectives of the whole business.

The technique known as 'management by objectives' (MbO) was developed in the 1960s and is central to the way many organizations continue to manage both their operations and their people. It follows a simple and logical sequence of steps:

1   Formulate strategic plans.
2   Develop tactical plans.
3   Develop unit plans.
4   Set key result areas and targets for individual managers.
5   Establish performance monitoring and control systems.

In fact, the process can be better understood as a control loop (see Figure 7.1).

Seen in this way, the performance of every individual manager is regularly compared with the contribution expected to the achievement of the organization's strategic plans.

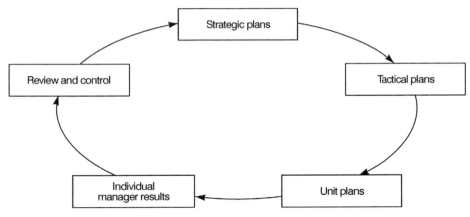

Figure 7.1   Management by objectives

First introduced over thirty years ago, MbO has been refined and updated over time. The first refinement has been a move away from the traditional cascade system of imposing objectives from the top to the more empowering approach of involving staff in the setting up of their own objectives, within the wider context of the organization's mission and goals. The second refinement has been to recognize that this approach is not limited to setting objectives for managers, but can be applied to everyone in the workforce.

Management by objectives techniques are often used to support performance appraisal (alternatively called the annual appraisal or the staff review system). At each level in the organization, managers discuss with their subordinates the 'key result' areas which the managers have already agreed with their own supervisors. Managers and subordinates then agree what the subordinates' key tasks are which will contribute to the achievement of those key results. The key tasks are then considered in terms of the performance standards to be achieved and the controls by which performance will be monitored.

As you would expect, standards should be quantitative and therefore measurable wherever possible, although the nature of some work may make it necessary to include judged or qualitative standards, where their achievement can be observed, though not measured.

The objectives used in this kind of standards-based performance appraisal are often said to need to be SMART:

- Specific
- Measurable
- Agreed
- Realistic
- Time-based.

In other words, the outputs expected from the individual should be clearly defined such that performance can be quantified, agreed with the individual, achievable within the constraints of time and resources and with a target date for achievement to be measured and compared.

At first sight, standards-based performance appraisal using SMART objectives provides an attractive way of linking individual performance to the achievement of corporate goals. Unfortunately, in many cases this approach proves less satisfactory in practice than it promises to be in theory. There are several reasons for this:

- No effective mechanism exists for cascading corporate goals down the organization.
- Insufficient attention is paid to ensuring that tactical and unit plans support corporate objectives.
- Managers have difficulty in translating expectations of individual performance into specific, measurable and time-based form.
- Managers are keener to maintain friendly relations with subordinates than they are to set challenging objectives. As a result, objectives reflect standards of performance which can be achieved with little or no effort.

CASE STUDY

A local government department in the North of England put together a business plan in line with national guidelines, local needs and the resources available to it. However, it failed to communicate the plan to its staff. Tasks and objectives agreed between managers and subordinates were based simply on the standards achieved in the previous year.

There is an extensive range of performance standards which can be applied to staff members. Here are some examples:

Sales force

- gross revenue per member
- profit per member
- weekly sales visits
- travel time v. contact time v. desk time
- product and market knowledge

- interview skills
- planning skills
- orders per member
- order size
- sales volume per call
- profit per call.

Production staff

- output per member
- materials waste
- machine downtime
- days off sick
- reject rates
- labour cost as percentage of output value
- improvements suggested.

Administration staff

- output per member
- error rate
- training undertaken
- computer literacy
- time taken to process enquiries
- days off sick.

Some of these are subject to quantitative measurement (sales, output, reject rates, error rates). Some can only be judged qualitatively (product knowledge, training undertaken). Nevertheless, all these performance indicators offer a firm basis on which to set objectives, provided the manager concerned has the courage both to make them challenging and to give an honest and accurate review of their achievement.

But, as we pointed out earlier, performance standards do not apply solely to people. Effective control of operations demands that every aspect of operations be monitored against relevant and, wherever possible, measurable standards.

In Chapter 5, we emphasized the need to carry out a careful analysis of the flow of inputs and outputs, the effectiveness of the transformation process at each stage of the operation and the quality of the resources, systems and procedures supporting it. At that point, we suggested the analysis as a starting point for quality improvement. However, the use of flow charts and process reviews will also highlight the critical points in the operation where particular performance standards must be achieved. Take the process flow chart in Figure 7.2 as an example.

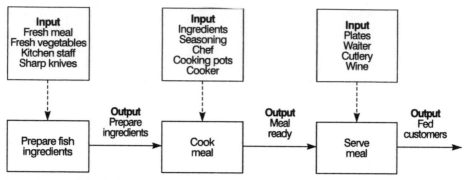

Figure 7.2   Simplified restaurant process flow chart

The success of each stage of the process is dependent on the quality and availability of the necessary inputs, whether they are raw materials or reusable resources. So, in order to set process performance standards, we need to ask some probing questions:

Prepare ingredients

- How regular and reliable are ingredient deliveries?
- Are sufficient kitchen staff available?
- Do they have the necessary skills?
- How often are the knives sharpened?
- How long does the preparation take?

Cook meal

- How often are stocks of seasoning, cooking oils, etc. checked?
- How effective is the system for reordering them?
- Does the chef have the necessary skills?
- Are there enough cooking pots?
- Is the cooker big enough, fast enough?
- How long does the cooking take?

Serve meal

- Are there enough plates and cutlery?
- Does the waiter have the necessary skills?
- How are the wine stocks controlled?
- How satisfactory is the replenishment system?
- How long does it take to serve?

The answers to these and other related questions will help identify the critical success factors for our restaurant process and provide the basis for the development of performance standards and control mechanisms. For example, if our restaurant has decided that one of its strategic aims is to enable customers to arrive, order, eat and leave within an hour, it will be necessary to set standards for preparation, cooking and serving times which make this possible. If the process is currently failing to meet those standards, then further action will be required to identify why not and to decide how to resolve the issue. But how, in this case, would performance be compared with the standards?

Performance monitoring can be applied to all cases, or to a sample. For example, a salesperson will submit details of all orders taken as part of the process of getting the orders fulfilled. As a result, the data necessary to monitor average order value or total weekly sales is already available. Consequently, it is relatively straightforward to monitor the total population – all sales by all salespeople.

Our restaurant is a different case. It would be unrealistic to expect the operations manager here – probably the owner, or the chef and head waiter taking responsibility for different stages of the process – to spend all their time with a stopwatch measuring preparation, cooking or serving time. Instead, it would give equally valid data to measure a sample, but only if the sample is statistically reliable. In other words, it must be representative of the total population. To achieve that, it would be advisable to measure performance

- at busy and quiet times of the day
- on different days of the week
- at different times of the year

if the restaurant is subject to seasonal variations in trade.

It would be equally necessary to measure the performance against the standard of the process when different staff are on duty, again to make sure the measures are truly representative.

However, all performance monitoring tells you is whether the performance is up to standard. If it is not, more work is needed to find out why not and to put it right. These are the subjects of our next two sections.

EVALUATING SHORTFALLS

In Chapter 9 we shall examine in detail two alternative approaches to problem-solving. For the moment, and as an introduction to that examination, we shall consider two simple techniques which are often used in business process re-engineering: the critical examination matrix and the fishbone diagram.

WHAT is done?	WHY is it done?	What ELSE could be done?	What else SHOULD be done?
HOW is it done?	WHY that way?	How ELSE could it be done?	How else SHOULD it be done?
WHEN is it done?	WHY then?	When ELSE could it be done?	When else SHOULD it be done?
WHERE is it done?	WHY there?	Where ELSE could it be done?	Where else SHOULD it be done?
WHO does it?	WHY them?	Who ELSE could do it?	Who else SHOULD do it?

Figure 7.3   Critical examination matrix

Critical examination matrix

The objective of this matrix is to provide a structured way of challenging every activity on the process flow chart. It asks the questions shown in Figure 7.3.

The great benefit of the matrix is that it makes no assumption and takes nothing for granted. Of course, it is time-consuming to use. Nevertheless, the thoroughness it brings to process analysis ensures that it highlights every possible cause of inefficiency:

- poor output specifications
- inadequate systems or procedures
- delays and waiting time
- excess transportation
- staff quality, skill, excess workload.

It does not, of course, indicate what answers you should expect. However, it is a valuable way of challenging those activities and approaches which somehow seem to creep into processes without anyone asking why – or, if someone does ask, can only be justified on historical grounds: 'but that's the way we've always done it'.

The Groundwork Foundation, a charity based in Birmingham, uses a complicated form of staff appraisal modelled largely on the Civil Service approach. This is because much of its funding comes from the Government and, when the appraisal system was introduced, it was felt that the Civil Service approach, including an element of performance-related pay, would be most acceptable to the Department of the Environment, which holds the purse-strings.

The system, however, is heavily paper-intensive and very time-consuming for both managers and staff. Government funding is also not adequate for performance-related pay awards to be meaningful. These factors have brought the system into disrepute.

The decision to introduce it was based on a historical misjudgement of what the Government would expect. Groundwork is now in the process of simplifying and reshaping the system, in order to make it more consistent with business needs and staff expectations.

Fishbone diagram

Known alternatively as a cause-and-effect diagram, this technique is a useful way of identifying the root cause of a problem – or, in the context of performance monitoring, the root cause of a discrepancy between performance and standard.

The technique is primarily a visual prompt for brainstorming. It involves drawing a fish skeleton with the problem or performance shortfall at the head and a framework of potential causes as the main bones leading from the backbone. You may choose simply to brainstorm and categorize those causes or, alternatively, to use the standard PEM/PEM prompts (People, Environment, Methods; Plant, Equipment, Materials) or else the 4M prompts: Men, Materials, Methods, Machinery. A fishbone diagram using PEM/PEM prompts is shown in Figure 7.4.

From here on, the technique simply keeps repeating the question 'why?' so, for example, you might start by asking: 'why might people be contributing to this performance shortfall?'

There could be several answers:

- Because there aren't enough of them.
- Because they don't have the necessary skills.
- Because no one has told them what standard is expected.

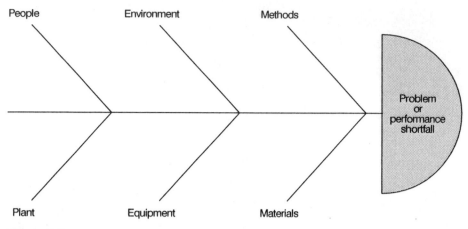

Figure 7.4

■   Because they don't know what standard they are achieving.

Each of these answers now forms a smaller bone to the main bone, headed 'People'. But the technique does not stop there. It takes the 'why?' question further:

■   Why aren't there enough people? Because we have a lot of unfilled vacancies.
■   Why do we have a lot of unfilled vacancies? Because we can't attract suitable people.
■   Why can't we attract suitable people? Because we don't pay as much as our competitors.

And so on. Ultimately this repeated questioning will lead you to the fundamental cause of the shortfall, at which point you can develop an action plan or solution to address the root cause, rather than just the symptoms you started with.

Figure 7.5 is a hypothetical fishbone diagram for a secondary school which has failed to achieve its performance target of GCSE passes at Grades A–C.

We would not suggest that the simple fact of identifying these causes makes them easy to solve. However, it does now make it possible for the school to:

■   separate causes which it can address (the internal factors) from those which are outside its control (high unemployment in the area, for example)

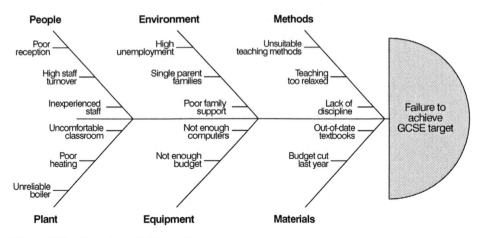

Figure 7.5   Completed fishbone diagram

- avoid unsuitable remedial action (for example, introducing more severe punishment for misbehaviour will be less effective in addressing lack of discipline than arranging for staff to be trained in more suitable teaching methods)
- differentiate between tactical solutions (raise funds to buy new textbooks) and those which require a more strategic approach (improving the school's reputation to attract more experienced staff).

This distinction between tactical and strategic solutions is the subject of the next section.

REMEDIAL ACTION: TACTICAL AND STRATEGIC

Even in the days of delegated responsibility and decision-making, it is not uncommon to come across operations managers who, having recognized shortfalls in performance and identified the causes, are still prevented either by their limits of authority or by lack of access to budget or for other reasons from taking remedial action. If this is your situation, then the best we can suggest is that you treat this as an environmental constraint imposed on you by the culture of your organization and take whatever action you can to influence the situation by working through your own line manager. Ways of doing this were suggested in Chapter 2 and I will return to this theme in Chapter 10.

In this section, we shall assume that you have the power and authority both to identify performance shortfalls and to take remedial action. Table 7.1 shows the results of performance monitoring carried out over a period of six months in a neighbourhood corner supermarket.

Table 7.1 Performance monitoring results

	1997 sales forecast £	1997 actual sales £	1996 actual sales £
January	8,100	7,900	7,900
February	8,500	8,300	8,200
March	8,500	8,400	8,200
April	9,200	7,200	9,000
May	9,200	7,400	9,000
June	8,700	6,300	8,500

It is obvious from the figures in Table 7.1 that the business is failing to meet its performance targets. It is also reasonable to assume that this failure is likely to have a serious impact on the owner's ability to pay rent, rates, overheads and staff costs.

What the figures do not explain, however, is the reason for the failure. Even from the figures above, though, we can hazard some guesses.

The owner appears to have predicted year-on-year growth of roughly 3 per cent. This looks reasonable and could simply be calculated on the basis of an inflation factor. But it leaves some important questions unanswered:

- What demographic changes have taken place in the neighbourhood? Has there been an increase in empty properties? Do local families have less money to spend this year? Or have some richer folk moved in, who travel by car to shops elsewhere?
- Have neighbourhood tastes changed? Are local people avoiding the shop because it no longer stocks the merchandise they want?
- Was the inflation factor accurate? Or does the owner buy from suppliers who are aggressively cutting retail prices?

None of these questions can be answered accurately from the performance data given. To do that will require further research and, possibly, the collection of some further data – population changes, perhaps, or a small-scale survey amongst customers to identify current preferences, or an examination of inflation rates.

Such approaches, together with the use of a brainstorming technique like the fishbone diagram, may highlight reasons why the original sales forecast was optimistic. It does not, however, change the fact that one form of remedial action, when faced with failure to meet a performance standard, may be to recognize that the standard was unachievable – and therefore devalues it!

CASE STUDY

In the aggressive 1960s and 1970s, the standard philosophy when it came to setting performance standards for salespeople was that, if the standards were achievable, salespeople would stop striving. Researching the phenomenon, however, occupational psychologists made the predictable discovery that salespeople got used to the idea that they were being set impossible targets and simply gave up taking any notice of them.

Other forms of remedial action at a tactical level may include:

- changing a supplier
- improving the output specification
- training the staff
- improving the available resources
- streamlining the process
- upgrading the machinery
- improving quality control
- consulting the customer
- consulting the supplier
- recruiting more staff
- improving maintenance
- upgrading facilities
- improving the input specification.

We deal with the practical details of carrying out these improvements in Chapters 8 and 9.

It is important to recognize, though, that not all performance shortfalls can be remedied by tactical action.

CASE STUDY

As is usual in wartime, junior officers in the British Army in France during the First World War were responsible for the morale of their men. However, morale was greatly reduced by poor food, lack of equipment and Headquarters decisions which self-evidently were wholly at variance with the reality seen from the trenches. As a result, junior officers were responsible for a performance standard which they had neither the authority nor the resources to influence.

One of the key lessons of operations management is the horizontal nature of the process and the consequent interdependence of teams and functions. This means that a decision taken in a far-off department, or at a higher level, may have a totally unanticipated impact on you.

CASE STUDY

In the 1980s the Fiat Motor Company took the decision to protect its cash flow by paying its suppliers as late as it could get away with. The Training Department wanted to have a small brochure typeset and printed locally. However, local printers were aware of the company's cash flow decision. As a result, none was prepared to take on the job.

The critical examination matrix and fishbone technique we described earlier should highlight problems, causes and performance shortfalls which are not susceptible to remedial action at a tactical level.

Having identified the need for a strategic solution – or one which is outside your own span of control – you have three options:

- sit tight and wait
- make do and mend
- find someone and shout.

Sit tight and wait

This option is only justifiable if you work in an organization where strategic plans and cross-team information flow easily and freely. In such an environment, you should know the strategic and other initiatives which are likely to have an impact on performance shortfalls you are currently facing. But, even then, you need to be realistic. Ask yourself:

- Will this initiative take effect early enough to solve my problem?
- How confident am I that it will have the favourable effect I am hoping for?
- I am not in control of it, so can I be sure it will really happen?

If your answers to those questions are positive, then it will be preferable to sit and wait, rather than taking local remedial action which will then be overtaken by events. On the other hand, if you cannot be so positive, then waiting for someone else to solve your problem for you is likely to prove risky.

CASE STUDY

Dudley Training and Enterprise Council is currently discussing possible collaboration or merger with two other local TECs. It is also carrying out a thorough review and overhaul of its human resource policies and practices. If the merger takes place, the new human resource policies will be redundant, because a different set will be needed for the merged business. However, a merger is not guaranteed. So the review continues.

If you cannot rely on a solution from elsewhere, it might be better to adopt a different option.

Make do and mend

You were earlier advised against dealing with symptoms rather than root causes. However, if the root cause concerning you can only be tackled by a strategic initiative – and you are uncertain about the timing or the efficacy of that initiative – then it is better to take local action to relieve some of the symptoms. The benefits will be:

- respect from your staff for grasping the difficulty
- a reduction, though probably not the elimination, of the problem
- an improvement in performance, though perhaps not full achievement of the standard.

Find someone and shout

This advice is not intended to be taken literally! Another term for the same idea, though, is networking. Networking involves finding other people either inside or outside the organization who have the power, authority or influence to bring about the changes you need so that you can improve your operation's performance. Then it involves establishing a relationship with those people based on mutual respect and co-operation. As Robert Townsend recommends in his book *Further Up the Organization* (Coronet, 1970): 'The head of the mail room or the chief telephone operator may hold your destiny someday. Figure out who's important to your effectiveness and then treat him (or her) that way.'

This approach is dependent on your sensitivity to the politics of your organization. You will need to be aware of who exerts both formal (hierarchical) and informal influence. Your objective is to find ways of supporting them, so that they will support you.

If the change you are seeking is strategic, or if the only way to gain support in your organization from someone in another function is by working through the hierarchy, then your key contact will be your own manager. In that case:

- Work out and present the operational and organizational benefits of the change.
- Explain how your manager will benefit from the change.
- Describe exactly what you want to happen.
- Present an action plan for implementation.

Before leaving the topic of remedial action, it is worth pointing out that a failure to achieve performance standards can take the form of overperformance as well as underperformance. The consequences of too much output can be as significant as not enough. For example:

- excess usage of inputs or raw materials
- exceeding customer demand
- excess wear on equipment or machinery.

As far as remedial action is concerned, overperformance can also have both tactical and strategic implications. At a strategic level, the first questions should be:

- Does the customer want this much output?
- Are they prepared to pay for it?

If the customer does not want the extra output, then remedial action may take the form of deciding how to use the surplus production capacity which is released by restricting output levels to those specified in the performance standard.

INVOLVING OTHERS

This section returns to a theme introduced earlier in this book – the importance of delegating decisions to those who will be affected by them.

As far as monitoring and control are concerned, this involves:

- making a clear connection between the different activities or processes which make up your operation and the individuals or teams responsible for them

- setting and agreeing individual or team performance targets
- instituting methods of performance measurement
- making performance data available to those responsible for achieving the targets
- ensuring you have access to individual or composite data
- agreeing responsibility and authority for remedial action
- monitoring the initiation, implementation and success of such action.

The rest of this section develops each of those activities in more detail.

Connecting individuals or teams

The process analysis described earlier in this book should have identified members of staff as one of the inputs to each transformation process. Two alternative steps are then possible, depending on your organization's culture and attitude to teamworking.

One alternative is to break down each process into activities small enough to be the responsibility of a single individual. This is likely to be the favoured approach in organizations staffed largely by knowledge workers, where each contribution is clearly differentiated or where individual performance pay is part of the reward package.

The other alternative is to connect processes with teams rather than individuals. This is likely to be found in organizations which have adopted a team or task culture, or which have gone down the quality circle route.

Agreeing performance targets

A technique for agreeing individual targets was described earlier in this chapter. Agreeing team targets is similar, except that it is then up to the team to decide amongst themselves what each individual will contribute to the achievement of the target.

Instituting performance measurement

Measurement methods may be manual or automated, based on quantitative or qualitative measures. Most organizations will have methods and measures designed for their own operations, although smaller businesses may choose to install a generic system. Care is necessary in doing this, because there is a significant risk that either the monitoring methods or the measures, or both, will be a poor fit with the needs of the business.

Making data available

A central aspect of empowerment is giving people feedback on their performance. The provision of performance data direct to staff is an effective way of doing this. However, it is important to avoid the trap of presenting the data in a form which is difficult to digest, interpret or understand. Managers around in the 1970s will remember having to wade through several inches of computer-generated statistical information each month just to find the three lines on page 327 (or whatever) that were relevant to them!

Access to data

Delegating monitoring and control does not mean abdicating responsibility for it. The operations manager may want to access the same data that are available to staff or, alternatively, to arrange to receive summary information which amalgamates the discrete elements.

Agreeing remedial action

Monitoring means measurement. Control means action. Monitoring and control go together. So it makes no sense to delegate the responsibility and not the authority to take the remedial action. However, we all need to know the nature and scope of the decisions we are entitled to take. Delegating authority will therefore involve setting limits to that authority, expressed perhaps in terms of:

- a budget
- specific processes or activities
- limits of impact on others.

Monitoring remedial action

The key to effective management has been described as 'no surprises'. In other words, as a manager, you do not want to be caught out by anything that anyone else does. Instead, you should anticipate and be ready for it. In part, that means you need to know when remedial action is necessary, whether it has been taken and how well it worked. Of course, initiation, implementation and monitoring have all been passed to your staff. However, that does not remove the need for regular progress reviews – informal discussion, 'walking the job', asking the right questions. If you think that sounds a little like watching your own back, I wouldn't argue.

COMPETENCE SELF-ASSESSMENT

1   What performance monitoring data is available to you?
2   How satisfactory is it? How could it be improved?
3   How closely do your and your staff's performance objectives reflect the objectives of your organization?
4   What would need to happen to bring them closer together?
5   How SMART are your objectives? How could they be improved?
6   What performance standards are in place for your staff? How could they be improved?
7   What process standards do you have in place? How could they be improved?
8   Prepare a fishbone diagram for a performance shortfall in your operation.
9   Identify the remedial action necessary to address the shortfall. Is that action tactical or strategic?
10 How could you involve your staff more in performance monitoring and control?

8 Continuous improvement

OBJECTIVES OF CONTINUOUS IMPROVEMENT

On an individual level, the search for continuous improvement appears to be part of our genetic conditioning. Just as fish developed legs and lungs in order to improve their chances of survival by moving onto the land, so today we seek to improve our personal situations by:

- gaining more qualifications
- moving into a bigger house
- making more friends
- achieving promotion
- boosting our reputations
- impressing the boss.

Arguably, through all these activities, we are following the Darwinian principle of 'the survival of the fittest'.

'Now hold on', interrupted the cynical accountant from our earlier debates. 'Darwin concluded that we improve in order to survive, not that we survive in order to improve. You seem to be suggesting that continuous improvement should be a way of life, regardless of need – or cost!'

There are two sides to the argument about continuous improvement. By some, it is promoted as the only justifiable approach to organizational life. Current systems and methodologies are never good enough. There is always a better way. The best is always around the corner.

Some organizations that have adopted continuous improvement as a watchword take this approach. However, it is at variance with the management gurus from the relevant literature:

> To maintain a wave of interest in quality, it is necessary to develop generations of managers who not only understand but are dedicated to the pursuit of never-ending improvement in meeting external and internal customer needs.
> (John S. Oakland, *Total Quality Management*, Butterworth-Heinemann, 1989)

> The need for innovation on an unprecedented scale is a given. The question is how. It seems that giving the market free rein, inside and outside the firm, is the best – perhaps the only – satisfactory answer.
> (Tom Peters, *Liberation Management*, Macmillan, 1992)

> Technology and economics is a potent blend. It is the premise to this book that from that blend all sorts of changes ensue.
> (Charles Handy, *The Age of Unreason*, Hutchinson, 1989)

> Processes are how the organization delivers outputs to the customer. The closer the fit between what the customer wants and what you deliver, the more successful you are likely to be in securing and retaining customers. But as we have seen, organizations are operating in an environment of constant change – in the marketplace, in their immediate environment, in technology, and, most importantly, in what their customers want and expect from them. It is not enough simply to keep an eye on existing processes and solve the occasional problem. The goal posts are moving; so it is a question of constantly readjusting your aim to stay on target.
> (Teresa Riley, *Understanding Business Process Management*, Pergamon, 1997)

'I'm all in favour of that', commented our marketing manager. 'If continuous improvement means bringing our products closer to what the customer wants, that makes my job easier. The products will be easier to promote. Customers will be more satisfied. Yes, I like that.'

The marketing manager is right, of course – but only up to a point. As you would expect from earlier contributions, he is missing important aspects of the total picture.

As pointed out earlier, continuous improvement is essential to organizational survival. But it is not simply to do with achieving a better fit between customer needs and the product or service provided by the operation, important though this is. In addition, continuous improvement is a process intended to:

- improve the match between the operation and the goals of the organization
- reduce costs
- increase efficiency
- reduce or eliminate waste
- increase job satisfaction.

'Ah, now you've got to it', broke in the personnel officer. 'In previous chapters of this book, you've gone on about the need to consult and involve staff. Well, believe me, not everyone finds continuous improvement satisfying. Improvement means change and, for a lot of people, change is difficult, unsettling. I'm all for increased job satisfaction – but don't pretend that continuous improvement is an unfailing route to it.'

This introduction to continuous improvement has put the topic into context. It is not simply a routine to be followed because that is the right way for up-to-date organizations to behave. Rather, it is a way of ensuring organizational survival by increasing customer satisfaction and competing more effectively. But only these two objectives are necessary to the survival of your organization. And continuous improvement is rarely painless – it brings risks, one of which is that of unsettling and alienating staff.

In the remainder of this chapter, we shall consider in greater detail:

- the needs for continuous improvement
- the risks of continuous improvement
- the process of continuous improvement
- the implications of continuous improvement.

Let us start with the arguments in favour.

THE NEED FOR CONTINUOUS IMPROVEMENT

The speed of change

The speed of environmental change – particularly in the areas of economics, society, technology and competition – is a recurring theme in management literature. A frequently quoted example is that of transport. As Figure 8.1 shows, from the dawn of time and for thousands of years, humankind was limited to travel on foot – and a maximum running speed of some 10 miles an hour. Catching and riding a horse, the invention of the wheel and the design of horse-drawn chariots and carriages doubled that speed. Then, in the nineteenth century, the invention of the steam engine revolutionized transport, in terms of both the speeds which could be reached and the distances which could be covered. The rapid development of the internal combustion engine brought about a dramatic acceleration in the speed of transport, accentuated by its use to power aeroplanes, followed by the invention of jet engines and the introduction of rocket travel. In less than two centuries, the speed of transport has increased from about 20 miles per hour to over twice the speed of sound.

Medical and biological technology offer similar examples. The twentieth century has seen the introduction of:

- open heart surgery
- organ transplants
- antibiotics

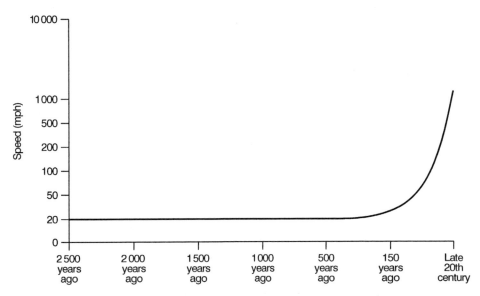

Figure 8.1 Rate of change in transport. Adapted from T. Riley, *Understanding Business Process Management*, Pergamon, 1997.

- animal cloning
- eyesight correction by laser treatment.

Social change has also been rapid during this century. For example:

- an increase in divorce rates
- a move away from marriage to living together
- a growing acceptance of homosexual couples
- an increase in single parent families
- couples starting families later in life
- a growth in home working.

All these changes have had a major impact on what is technically possible in operations management and on customer expectations and market demands. Add to that increased industrialization in economies like those of India and the countries of the Pacific Rim, the growth of multinational companies and increased diversification, and the consequences for changes in competition are self-evident.

CASE STUDY

Tom Peters quotes the following from the preface to *Liberation Management* (Macmillan, 1992):

Recently I was talking to one of Japan's best foreign-exchange dealers, and I asked him to name the factors he considered in buying and selling. He said, 'Many factors, sometimes very short-term, and some medium, and some long-term'. I became very interested when he said he considered the long term and asked him what he meant by that time frame. He paused a few seconds and replied with genuine seriousness: 'Probably ten minutes.' That is the way the market is moving these days.

It is obvious from all this that, as customer needs, wants and expectations are changing, available technology is changing, markets are changing and competitors and the nature of competition are changing, so organizations and operations need to change in response.

Continuous and discontinuous change

We need to distinguish here between two different types of change:

- continuous or incremental change
- discontinuous change.

Recent management literature has placed considerable emphasis on the need to respond effectively to discontinuous change. Charles Handy in *The Age of Unreason* (Hutchinson, 1989) starts his book by writing:

> The story or argument of this book rests on three assumptions:
>
> - that the changes are different this time: they are discontinuous and not part of a pattern; that such discontinuity happens from time to time in history, although it is confusing and disturbing, particularly to those in power
> - that it is the little changes which can in fact make the biggest differences to our lives, even if these go unnoticed at the time, and that it is the changes in the way our *work* is organized which will make the biggest difference to the way we all will *live*
> - that discontinuous change requires discontinuous upside-down thinking to deal with it, even if both thinkers and thoughts appear absurd at first sight.

The proposition behind this emphasis on discontinuous change is that we can no longer predict the future by extrapolating from the present and the past. Past solutions will not be relevant to future problems. Hence Handy's reference to the need for 'upside-down thinking'. Of course, failures to recognize discontinuous change have proved a major threat to many organizations.

CASE STUDY

IBM failed to notice the rapidly growing power and user-convenience of personal computers (PCs), preferring to remain with the mainframes which had traditionally been a totally reliable source of profit. They introduced PCs five years later, following a dramatic drop in mainframe sales which almost crippled the business.

The significance of discontinuous change on operations will be drastic – and significantly disruptive. It is likely to require:

- retooling and re-equipping to produce new products
- the recruitment of new staff and retraining of existing staff to introduce new services
- the abandonment of old systems and their replacement with new systems
- the adoption of new philosophies and new attitudes
- a redefinition of markets and customers
- entry into new markets and the abandonment of old markets.

Chapter 9 deals in more detail with responses to discontinuous change.

Risk management

Responses to continuous or incremental change are the central theme of continuous improvement. Nevertheless, there are some basic principles which underpin both sets of responses. Vincent Nolan in his book *The Innovator's Handbook* (Sphere, 1987) relates change and improvement to the issue of risk. He explains:

Probably the most important difference between innovative and routine management lies in the attitudes toward and the handling of risks. The risks of innovation are of two quite different kinds: alongside the risks of something actually going wrong in the real world, is the emotional risk of being criticized or blamed, feeling foolish or embarrassed.

The interaction of these two types of risk (which for convenience I will label 'subjective' and 'objective') enables us to identify four different categories of risky situations, as follows:

Low Subjective/Low Objective
Feels low risk, and is in fact low risk, because the familiar methods are still appropriate – call it ROUTINE

High Subjective/Low Objective
Feels risky, because it is something I have not done before, but even if it turns out badly, the outcome is tolerable and affordable because it is a low risk experiment – call it EXPERIMENTAL

Low Subjective/High Objective
Feels safe, because it is familiar, but in fact is high risk, because the situation has changed and the old ways are no longer appropriate. Call it the OSTRICH position

High Subjective/High Objective
Feels risky, and is in fact high risk. It's a GAMBLE

The well managed business operates mainly in the lower half of the diagram below [see Figure 8.2], moving between the Routine and the Experimental (spiced, perhaps, with the occasional, affordable Gamble). It makes money from its Routine activities; it innovates and safeguards its future through the results of its Experimental work.

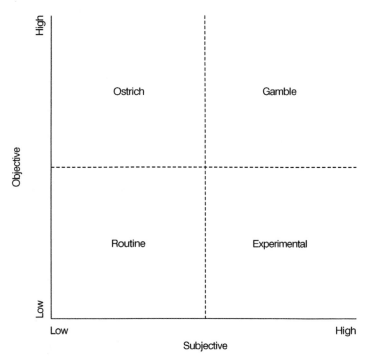

Figure 8.2

Similarly the individual manager will maintain a mix of routine and experimental activities, the routine providing a basis of productive output and the experimental pushing out the frontiers and new possibilities ...

> By contrast, the business or individual who never experiments and continues to do things 'the way we've always done it' feels safe and comfortable but is in fact taking a big risk of being caught out by changing circumstances ...
>
> There then tends to be a panic reaction, an urgent need for drastic new action, without a bank of experimental learning and experimental skills to draw upon. The result is often a Gamble – a great leap forwards, into major new initiatives, untried and untested, with no groundwork of knowledge or experience.

Nolan's argument is an important one. It is that continuous improvement (which he calls 'experimentation') is an essential preparation for managing discontinuous change (the 'gamble') because:

- Continuous improvement reduces the need for 'great leaps' into the unknown.
- Continuous improvement is a valuable way of developing the knowledge, skills and confidence necessary for innovation.

Both points are crucial. As our personnel officer pointed out earlier, people find change uncomfortable and unsettling. Getting them to love change is probably unrealistic. However, developing an environment and a culture in which change is a way of life, where attempts to improve efficiency, effectiveness and responsiveness are welcomed, encouraged and supported, will go a long way to removing the fear of change and the unwillingness to experiment.

CASE STUDY

Talk to anyone in government service and they will complain about what has come to be known as 'initiative fatigue'. This refers to the fact that, in the last decade, civil servants have been bombarded with changes to priorities, working practices, philosophies and the terms and conditions of employment. Many will state emphatically that 'this isn't the organization I joined'.

The main trouble is that the current multiplication of change initiatives has followed generations of stability, even stagnation. Instead of implementing a long-term process of incremental change, civil servants are now being asked to respond to major discontinuous change, to which they are not accustomed and which is inconsistent with the expectations they brought when they joined.

The need for information

However, this does not change the fact that continuous improvement is essential to organizational survival. But if operations managers are to make continuous improvements which are genuine improvements, rather than irrelevant tweaks to the transformation process, they need to know:

- What are the priorities and main objectives of my organization currently?
- How much do I really know about the wants and needs of internal and external customers?
- How satisfied are they with the outputs for which I am responsible?
- What are my productivity and efficiency targets?
- How likely are my current operating processes to achieve them?
- What should be my priorities for improvement?
- What authority do I currently have to implement changes?
- If my authority is not consistent with the improvements I want to make, how can I increase it?
- Alternatively, to whom should I submit proposals for improvement?

Ways of answering some of these questions are dealt with later in the chapter. Chapter 7 examines ways of monitoring efficiency, effectiveness and responsiveness and Chapter 10 will look at the issues of authority and authorization. So, for the moment, we shall leave the topic of why continuous improvement is necessary, in order to deal with the risks inherent in it.

RISKS OF CONTINUOUS IMPROVEMENT

'Creative dissatisfaction' – good or bad?

It is often argued that effective managers should be continuously subject to 'creative dissatisfaction'. In other words, they should resist the temptation to leave things alone, just because they seem to be working all right. The argument is that most, if not all, operations and purposes are suboptimal in performance – they could be better, if only someone would actively seek improvements.

The opposite argument can be summarized in the American catch-phrase: 'If it ain't bust, don't fix it'. The obvious implication of this is that seeking improvement where there is no obvious need for it stands a good chance of making things worse, not better.

CASE STUDY

Caius Petronius, a Roman centurion, wrote in AD 66:

We trained hard, but it seemed that every time we were beginning to form up into teams, we would be re-organized. I was to learn later in life that we tend to meet any new situation by re-organizing, and a wonderful method it can be for creating the illusion of progress while producing confusion, inefficiency and demoralization.

Confusion, inefficiency, demoralization

The case study quoted highlights three of the risks of any improvement initiative:

- Those involved in implementing it will be confused if the reasons for it are not communicated, explained and justified.
- Change involves inefficiency, at least in the short term, as the new process or system is introduced, the shortfalls identified and the process debugged.
- People are often demoralized as they are forced to give up old operating methods with which they were familiar and which they took pride in making work, only to introduce new methods which prove inefficient and troublesome.

All three of these risks apply to any change initiative, whether it is a matter of revolution (major change) or evolution (continuous improvement). But there are more:

What further risks are inherent in continuous improvement?

We believe there are three, although each is significant enough to have several manifestations.

Irrelevance

The first, quite simply, is irrelevance. It was pointed out earlier that any continuous improvement process can only be justified in terms of its contribution to one of the following:

- increased customer satisfaction
- the achievement of corporate goals
- cost reduction
- efficiency improvement
- the elimination of unproductive work
- the reduction or elimination of waste
- increased job satisfaction.

CASE STUDY

A team of overseas observers was invited to watch an artillery demonstration by a British Army gun crew. As the crew took up its positions, one of the observers asked: 'What is the purpose of that soldier standing to attention over there?'

His host replied: 'He's there to hold the horses.'

The battalion concerned had been mechanized for over fifty years.

Arguably, removal of the soldier would have reduced costs, improved efficiency, eliminated unproductive work and increased job satisfaction by allowing him to transfer to more meaningful work. His removal would have been a classic example of continuous improvement, responding to technological change.

The next case study exemplifies the opposite – 'continuous improvement' which makes no contribution to anything, in fact, just the reverse!

A local government department in the West Midlands has attempted to improve internal communications by the introduction of electronic mail. This has incurred significant development and implementation costs. At the same time, the department has dispensed with management briefings, on the basis that these would be a duplication of effort.

In fact, staff now complain that they have no idea what is going on. In some cases, this is because senior management fail to put strategic decisions onto electronic mail. In other cases, it is because staff fail to access information which is on the system.

QUESTION

How well does this initiative achieve the objectives for continuous improvement we set out just now?

Briefly, we would suggest that the results of the initiative are:

- reduced customer satisfaction, in so far as the staff feel they are told less than before
- as an attempt to achieve the corporate goal of improved internal communication, it has failed
- the cost of developing and implementing the system was probably higher than that of regular management briefings
- efficiency has deteriorated – staff know less
- the work involved in developing and implementing the system has been unproductive
- the effect of up-dating the information on the system is largely wasted, because staff do not access it
- staff are dissatisfied.

Overall, not a success!

Overambition

Our second risk inherent in continuous improvement is that of overambition or, put differently, it is the risk of assuming that you, as the operations manager, have access to the resources necessary to bring about the improvement you have identified.

Resources take many forms. Traditionally, they have been categorized as 'the four Ms':

- manpower
- money
- machinery
- motivation

although the first is now politically incorrect!

Nevertheless, this provides a useful breakdown. It also raises important questions for the operations manager in the implementation of continuous improvement:

- Do you have enough staff to maintain the required level of outputs, whilst undergoing the disruption of changing processes?
- Do they have the skills and attitudes necessary to seek and implement improvement?
- Is there any space in your budgets?
- What additional capital items can you afford?
- What freedom do you have to change revenue expenditure?
- How flexible is the equipment you currently use?
- What changes to its usage are you entitled to make?
- What can you do about out-of-date or worn-out machinery?
- Will attempts at improvement be welcomed or seen as a threat?
- Do your staff want to be involved in improvement – or do they see it as a threat?
- Are you in favour of continuous improvement?
- Or opposed to it?

Internal disruption

Our third risk is implied in what we have already said about meeting the needs of internal customers and operations management as a horizontal process or seamless web. It is the risk of internal disruption.

Coutts Development Consulting has recently introduced a new paperwork system for administrating its freelance consultants. The system requires consultants to use Coutts' own forms for claiming fees and expenses. Whilst not a major inconvenience, this is contrary to freelance consultants' normal method of raising their own invoices.

You may feel that causing aggravation to suppliers is not of great significance. After all, if you are paying them, they should do as they are told and be grateful.

QUESTION

What are the dangers of this attitude?

There are three dangers. First, in situations like this, customers are dependent on suppliers. It is dangerous to antagonize them to the point where you risk losing their support. Secondly, and returning to a point we made in Chapter 4, the consultants are customers too. Working on a freelance basis, they have the freedom to work for other clients. Finally, is the system efficient? It may be efficient for Coutts, but it certainly is not for the consultants – particularly when it comes to raising income tax returns! So, in terms of overall efficiency, is this a good idea?

Let us widen the discussion. If, as an operations manager, I or my team invent a way of improving a process, thereby improving efficiency and reducing costs in our section, what should I do if that improvement makes my customer's life more difficult?

The philosophy of total quality management would respond that customer satisfaction is the primary consideration. So internal efficiency and cost reduction are less important than meeting customer needs. In the context of the external customer, this is almost certainly true. But, when we consider internal customers, it is important to remember that we all work for the same organization. By extension, therefore, decisions about continuous improvement should be taken with reference to the organization's strategic aims and objectives or, in other words: what's best for the business as a whole?

So, how do we reconcile the different objectives we set out earlier for continuous improvement? That is part of the theme of the next section.

THE PROCESS OF CONTINUOUS IMPROVEMENT

Assessing the need

As we have already explained, the first stage of continuous improvement must be to work out whether there is any point in it, or in more detail:

- Is any improvement necessary?
- How much would improvement contribute?
- What cost is justifiable?

The answers to these questions are partly qualitative, partly quantitative.

Is any improvement necessary?

Few operations (if any) are perfect. All managers and all staff are fully capable of pointing out frustrations, stupidities, duplications, irrelevancies and waste. So, there is always room for improvement. Or is there? At this point, we would like to publish a couple of health warnings.

The first is a logical development of our quotation from Caius Petronius earlier in this chapter: all change leads to short-term inefficiency. As a result, it is important to recognize and quantify the short-term impact of change, in order to establish whether the short-term disruption is worthwhile and, secondly, to identify what action will be necessary in terms of, for example, staff consultation, training, replacement or additional equipment.

The second health warning is implicit in the advice 'if it ain't bust, don't fix it' quoted earlier. Faced with a problem, managers always have the choice to implement remedial action or to do nothing. Doing nothing is neither abdication nor admission of failure, provided that the decision has been taken deliberately and after consideration. There will be situations where the effort and resources needed to resolve the problem are more costly than the loss of output or quality which results from maintaining current operational processes.

How much would improvement contribute?

Continuous improvement may take the form of:

- eliminating duplication. For example, both the accounts department and line managers keeping records of expenditure.
- eliminating redundant steps. For example, repacking raw materials into smaller quantities if the process could be redesigned to accommodate the supplier's quantities, or if the supplier can deliver in smaller quantities.

- smoothing the process. For example, by reducing the number of times inputs or outputs need to be handed on from one operation to another.
- improving the layout. For example, by reducing the distances between sequential activities.
- processing in parallel. For example, by using network analysis, as we described in Chapter 3, in order to identify operational processes which could take place at the same time, thus reducing total duration.
- making the process more automated or introducing more sophisticated equipment. This need not be costly. A gas appliance installer reduced installation times by an average of 30 per cent by providing its engineers with plier wrenches, which are quicker to adjust than the adjustable spanners they had used previously.

Any of these improvements would appear superficially desirable. However, it is important to ask:

- What are the nature and scale of the resulting benefits?
- Does the improvement bring drawbacks of its own? For example, if you discontinue your own expenditure records, does the accounts department take so long to publish its own that it will be too late to take remedial action when needed?
- What will be the impact on the next activity or operation in the chain? For example, if you increase output by streamlining your operation, will this simply mean producing more inputs for the next operation than they can handle?

What cost is justifiable?

This question can be answered by calculating the short-term and long-term costs of the improvement in terms of money, time, effort and resources, and comparing them with the analysis of contribution and benefits we have just described.

Designing the improvement

Even if you have not involved your team in assessing the need for improvement – and it is normally good practice to involve them – it is essential that they should be at least consulted and ideally fully responsible for designing it.

CASE STUDY

The human resource strategy of Dudley Training and Enterprise Council states:

We recognize that the competence and experience of our staff entitle them to contribute to the planning process and to both understand and be involved in business decisions which affect them ... The TEC undertakes to delegate tactical decisions to those responsible for implementing them insofar as this is possible within the constraints of what is possible operationally.

The last part of this statement reflects the obvious fact that any organization operates within a framework of:

- budgetary constraints
- resource constraints
- corporate objectives and targets
- organizational values.

These are likely to set limits to the types and scope of improvement staff can realistically expect to implement. Staff need to know in advance from their manager or team leader what those limits are. Nothing is more demotivating than to be encouraged to seek improvements, only to be told at the end of the process that they are not affordable, or that the necessary resources cannot be made available, or that they are not in line with the business plan.

There are several ways of involving staff in process improvement. They may operate as:

- improvement project teams, brought together specially for that purpose
- cross-functional teams, with representatives from customer or supplier functions, or support or advisory functions like finance or marketing.
- quality teams, in organizations which have already implemented TQM, where the team remains constant and meets regularly to take on different issues.

In all of these teams, effective teamworking and successful outcomes are dependent on a number of key factors.

Clear objectives

It is important that teams should know, and be regularly reminded of, the objectives they are seeking to achieve. Depending on the nature of the team, these may be set by management or it may be part of the team's responsibility to decide its current priority. The latter approach is more time-consuming, but has been shown to gain greater commitment, provided that the team is well led, disciplined and has the necessary problem-solving skills.

Meeting rules

Team members need a general idea of how frequently they will meet, at what time of day and how long the meeting will last. Individual meetings will benefit from an agenda circulated in advance, with details of any work to be done or papers to be read ahead of the meeting.

Meetings will need a chairperson, a secretary and an agreed set of principles by which to operate. These should include:

- how formal or informal the meetings are to be
- a recognition of everyone's right to be heard
- the team's authority to, for example, co-opt others or require action
- how decisions will be taken (unanimity, majority vote, whether the chairperson has a casting vote)
- the use of problem-solving and decision-making techniques such as brainstorming and the statistical evaluation of options.

Allocating action

Improvement project teams normally operate to a fixed schedule and disperse when the project has been completed. To achieve deadlines, it is normal for these teams to allocate follow-up action to individual members between meetings.

Quality teams are permanent. Consequently it may be too time-consuming to expect follow-up action from individuals, although this does sometimes happen.

Where teams do allocate action to individuals, it is important to ensure that the workload is shared fairly between members and that there is a general recognition that the completion of allocated action is compulsory, not optional.

Teamworking

By definition, improvement teams need to be creative. It is a responsibility of both the team leader and the members to:

■ encourage and support creativity
■ listen to and build on others' ideas
■ allow for differences in views
■ reserve judgement
■ avoid personal criticism.

Further aspects of teamworking include reliable attendance, time-keeping, the completion of allocated actions and a willingness to contribute.

Process and progress reviews

It is advisable for teams regularly to set time aside to review both how successfully they are working together and the progress they are making.
Process reviews should cover:

■ levels and standards of individual contributions
■ interpersonal relationships
■ team co-operation.

Progress reviews should cover:

■ achievements against milestones and deadlines
■ relevance of action and success to date
■ progress towards final objectives.

Implementing the improvement

Depending on the nature of the team, this may or may not be part of their responsibility. Ideally, though, it should be, for two reasons:

■ Team members have the best understanding of the decisions they have taken and the intentions behind them.
■ It is a source of considerable personal satisfaction to put in place an improvement you have designed – and see it work.

It is rare, though, for implementation to be possible totally without support from others.
Project and cross-functional teams are likely to be dependent on other teams and colleagues for implementation of at least part of the improvement. To ensure co-operation and effective implementation it is important to:

■ communicate at the start the reasons for and objectives of the project, to gain commitment

- issue regular up-dates on progress
- consult regularly on issues which will impact on others
- give clear guidance on implementation
- monitor and supervise.

CASE STUDY

Malcolm Field, then the Managing Director of W. H. Smith, commented to the Company Training Manager: 'Management training costs me £3 million a year. What exactly am I getting for my money?'

The management team, after recovering from the shock, worked as a project team to find a way of quantifying the outcomes from management training. The resulting solution was a sophisticated form of measured performance assessment, carried out both before and after training and the measures compared.

Unfortunately, the project team failed to consult either its customers or its trainers. As a result, the customers neither understood nor supported the initiative and the trainers were very unenthusiastic.

Quality teams will normally require the support of their team leader or manager when it comes to implementing improvement. As we have pointed out, improvement brings short-term disruption and normally requires resources. Even in these days of empowerment – a theme to which we shall return in Chapter 10 – it is unusual for quality teams to have the authority to allow even a temporary drop in output, quality or efficiency, or to acquire the additional resources necessary.

Monitoring the improvement

The final stage in the continuous improvement process is to monitor the results arising from it. However, this should not be seen as an add-on, to be handled when all the other stages have been completed. Instead, monitoring systems should be a factor for consideration at the design stage and should continue to be a driving force throughout the rest of the process.

Monitoring in its broader applications was covered in Chapter 7. Here, I shall simply make some brief comments related to improvement monitoring. The first will already be familiar, since it relates to the need for quantified measures.

As Lord Kelvin said: 'If you cannot measure that of which you speak, and express it as a number, your knowledge is meagre and unsatisfactory.' This does not mean limiting the things you monitor to those you can count – units produced, machine utilization, volume of waste, for example. These are important, but only half the story. In addition, it is necessary to measure improvement in terms which do not lend themselves so readily to numbers – customer satisfaction, for example, or staff morale. However, as explained in Chapter 2, it is possible to quantify such factors by developing conversion charts which translate qualitative factors into quantities – although the process is slightly arbitrary.

Quantification is essential because of our next point. Improvement monitoring is a comparative process. It involves comparing the results actually achieved with:

- the objectives for the project
- historical results and, sometimes,
- external or internal benchmarks, to identify whether there is further need or scope for improvement.

Of course, numbers offer the only satisfactory way of making comparisons.

Which brings us to our final point about monitoring improvement. Continuous improvement, by definition, is a never-ending process. At the same time, performance monitoring of any kind is only worthwhile if it leads to remedial action where this is necessary.

The consequent danger is that so many improvement initiatives are going on at the same time, or following each other in such quick succession, that it becomes impossible to identify the source of the results you are monitoring. After each initiative it is better to let each change settle long enough to get a clear picture of the improvement resulting from it. Otherwise, you may know that something has worked, but you will have little idea of what it was.

IMPLICATIONS OF CONTINUOUS IMPROVEMENT

Continuous improvement is a little like dropping a pebble into a pond. As the ripples spread, they shake the reeds, disturb the ducks, splash the paddler on the other side and, possibly, capsize a little child's toy boat!

The theme of this section is the need to consider carefully the impact of continuous improvement on the various stakeholders of an organization. Such impact will vary in importance – sometimes it will be major, sometimes minor. It may be planned and intentional, or unintended and unexpected. It may be positive – or negative. Careful analysis is necessary to ensure that all impact is intentional and beneficial.

An organization's stakeholders can be defined as: all those parties to whom an organization owes a responsibility or duty of care. Or even, more cynically: all individuals and groups which can exert any influence over the organization.

The following list is representative:

Contractual stakeholders

- shareholders
- employees/voluntary workers
- customers/clients (both internal and external)
- members (in the case, for example, of a club, professional institute or motoring organization)
- suppliers
- lenders.

Other stakeholders

- government
- regulators
- electorate
- general public
- pressure groups
- media.

Your organization may define its stakeholders more narrowly. Indeed, some older management texts limit stakeholders to the owners of the business, specifically the shareholders. However, more recent management authors adopt the wider definition, which also has greater relevance for public and not-for-profit organizations.

Earlier in this chapter, the first stage in continuous improvement was described as being the assessment of need, and one element of that stage as the identification of benefits and drawbacks. The following case study shows how apparent benefits may be balanced by drawbacks.

CASE STUDY

Didcot Power Station ceased to bring in coal by train and transferred to road haulage. This operational decision was taken to reduce costs.

However, the decision overlooked, or chose to ignore, the impact on the community and other road-users. Buildings and washing on lines were all covered in coal dust, whilst roads past the station were clogged with slow-moving lorries.

The result was a succession of expensive and disruptive protests, although the decision remained unchanged.

So what impact would continuous improvement initiatives have on stake-holders? Here are some examples, chosen at random:

■ Increased efficiency leading to faster throughput may require extra or more frequent supplier deliveries.
■ Simpler order documentation may require staff in internal customer departments to be retrained.
■ Improved output specifications may necessitate different components or raw materials from suppliers.
■ A design consultancy may find its clients unable to respond quickly enough to draft copy or illustrations.
■ A utility company which increases its efficiency and sends out bills earlier may find that customers pay as before, resulting in more overdue accounts.
■ Improved systems may be more efficient, but are inconsistent with supplier or customer systems.
■ Improvements carried out for internal benefit may be unacceptable to external customers.

CASE STUDY

The hospitals in Oxford decided to increase revenue by charging outpatients and visitors for car parking. As a result, many now use the (free) staff car parks. In consequence, staff car parks are often full and it has been necessary to introduce vehicle clamping to reduce the problem.

In all of these examples, initiatives have turned out to lead to less improvement than intended, because of failure to foresee the full consequences.

There is not enough space here to explore fully all the possible implications of continuous improvement as it affects you. However, we can offer a summary in the form of a series of questions.

What are the implications of a continuous improvement initiative in terms of:

■ systems compatibility?
■ customer acceptance?
■ supplier responsiveness?
■ product or service compatibility?
■ workforce acceptance?
■ training needs?
■ recruitment or redundancy?

- environmental impact?
- community acceptance?
- media response?
- investor response?
- component or raw material needs?
- equipment needs?

Some of these questions apply to operations at a macro level, others to operations at a micro level, yet others to both. At first sight, some improvement initiatives may seem so minor that their impact on stakeholders will be minimal. In such cases, it is worth remembering the ripples in the pond.

COMPETENCE SELF-ASSESSMENT

1   Does your organization pay as much attention to continuous improvement as it should to ensure its survival? How about you personally?

2   How much environmental change is your organization experiencing? And your operation?

3   How much do you know about your organization's priorities, objectives and chosen markets?

4   What authority do you have to implement continuous improvement? Whose agreement do you need?

5   How could you create a climate where your staff would support continuous improvement?

6   Who do you consult about continuous improvement? Your staff? Your boss? Internal customers? Internal suppliers? Anyone else?

7   How do you assess the need for improvement? What else could you do?

8   Does your organization use improvement teams? If so, how could they be made more effective?

9   How do you monitor improvement? What more could you do?

10 Who are your organization's and your own stakeholders? How could you improve the way you consider the impact of improvement on them?

9 Managing change

In the last chapter, the need for a cautious approach to continuous improvement and the potential pitfalls inherent in the process were emphasized. In particular, I pointed out:

- the need to balance costs and benefits
- the dangers of excess enthusiasm
- the impact of employee resistance
- the possibility that product or service improvements may not be welcomed by the next customer in the value chain.

So, does that mean that the larger-scale operation of managing change is less fraught with those risks? Unfortunately, no. In fact, if continuous improvement demands careful handling, the need for care in managing revolutionary, rather than evolutionary, change is even greater.

'I told you so', commented our personnel officer. 'I said that people don't like change. It makes them feel uncomfortable. It's all very well to talk about the survival of the fittest – but how do you think the dinosaurs felt about that? Change means threat, however carefully you manage it. People are afraid they won't be able to cope, won't be able to adapt.'

'Yes, but', broke in the marketing manager, 'you can't just ignore the need for change. If we're not competitive, or fail to keep our products in line with customer requirements, or don't keep up with environmental change, then we're not going to survive. Business history is littered with dinosaurs. Think of the Sinclair C5 – that little three-wheeled electric car. Nobody wanted it – and it died. Or bespoke suits – high street tailors couldn't compete on price or delivery with the ready-made variety. How many tailors do you see these days outside Savile Row – and they compete in a different market! Or the old American gas-guzzler automobiles. They evolved too slowly to respond to change in the fuel market, so they lost out to European and Japanese cars. The message is right, you know – adapt or die.'

Our production manager felt trapped in the middle again. He could see the force of both arguments. He had experienced disruption when the factory had introduced new shift-work arrangements – and seen the resentment on the faces of his team. But he could also recognize the resultant cost savings and the need to increase output in line with customer demand. So who was right?

That question is answered in the remainder of this chapter. In it, I shall:

- present two approaches to problem-solving; the analytical or remedial on the one hand and the creative on the other. The first is more likely to identify the need for small-scale changes; the second to highlight opportunities for revolutionary improvement. Between them, they go some way to quantifying the size, scope and implications of change.

- examine the organization pressures which are likely to promote change, and those likely to resist it. Taken together, those two sets of pressures will help you identify the actions necessary to bring about effective change. This process is called force-field analysis.

- deal with the human factors of change by exploring what makes people fearful of or threatened by change; and discussing what can be done to help staff, if not to love change, then at least to accept and feel ownership of it.

APPROACHES TO PROBLEM-SOLVING

Effective problem-solving requires answers to the following ten questions:

- What is the current situation?
- What is wrong with it?
- What has caused the problem?
- What are its longer-term consequences?
- To whom is it important?
- How would things look if the problem were resolved?
- What are the alternative solutions?
- How much would each cost?

- Which provides the best fit with the problem?
- How can it be implemented?

These questions are all consistent with both the analytical and the creative approaches to which we have already referred.

The first, analytical, approach is characterized by the technique advanced by C. H. Kepner and B. B. Tregoe in their book *The Rational Manager* (McGraw-Hill, 1965). Kepner and Tregoe define a problem as 'a deviation from the norm'. Analytical problem-solving emphasizes the use of quantitative measures to identify the nature, resulting cost and consequent seriousness of a problem, and to evaluate potential solutions. Developed in the 1950s and 1960s (a period of relative stability and predictability), the analytical approach is based on the assumption that there is 'one best way' of doing things and that problem-solving is a process of identifying what that one best way should be and removing any obstacles to achieving it.

The creative approach to problem-solving, by contrast, defines a problem as 'the gap between where we are and where we want to be'. This definition, used by Vincent Nolan in *Problem Solving* (Sphere Books, 1987), is again typical of its period, in that it emphasizes a search for the ideal, thinking the unthinkable, the idea that perfection is just around the corner. Unlike the analytical approach, which acknowledges and acts within given limitations – of time, resources and budget, for example – creative problem-solving encourages us to disregard limitations and 'reach for the stars'.

Your reactions to these two alternative approaches to problem-solving will have been indicative of the organizational environment in which you operate. If your organization is risk-averse, discourages experimentation and either longs for or genuinely operates within a stable environment, you will probably have felt much more sympathy with the analytical approach. Even if your organization is tentative in its outlook and you feel frustrated by it, you may still feel that analytical problem-solving is the only safe route for you to follow.

Alternatively, if creative problem-solving was ringing bells for you, that probably means that your organization is facing major environmental challenges and has decided to risk some large-scale leaps into the unknown.

In either case, it is worth giving some serious thought to the ten questions we raised earlier.

What is the current situation?

In the language of analytical problem-solving, this may be a deviation from the norm in the shape of a difference between a historical pattern (identified by the kind of monitoring described in Chapter 7 of this book) and current performance.

> ### CASE STUDY
>
> Mentmore, the plastics-moulding company best known for Platignum pens but now a major supplier of components to Electrolux, Black and Decker and BT, established that it had suffered an unacceptable fall in profits which threatened shareholder returns. Further research revealed that this had resulted from entering into a single, but large, contract with a key customer which had been incorrectly costed. The question was: what to do about it?

Or, in the language of creative problem-solving, the current situation may be a gap between where we are and where we want to be in the shape of an inability to perform to the standards now expected by our customers, or imposed on us by our competition.

> ### CASE STUDY
>
> As the name suggests, Radio Rentals entered the market as a renter of home entertainment equipment which, at the time, was both too unreliable and too expensive for customers to buy. As the equipment became more reliable and retail prices fell, Radio Rentals found itself facing intense competition from shops offering similar equipment for sale. The company took the decision to diversify into both equipment sales and the rental of more complex items, dependent on more frequent maintenance (such as the early generations of home computers and domestic freezers).

What is wrong with it?

In both these examples, the answer to this question is, with hindsight, obvious. Mentmore had lost profit, Radio Rentals was losing market share. In other situations, the answer is less obvious:

- An increase in staff turnover may result in higher recruitment costs and reduced efficiency.
- An increase in machine downtime may result in lower output and higher unit costs.
- A lack of sales staff may result in lost sales or reduced customer satisfaction (all examples of variations from the norm).

- 'All anyone does around here is complain' is a statement which suggests low productivity and poor morale.
- 'We're the retailer of last resort' suggests unreliable turnover and profit, and a poor reputation with customers.
- 'All this organization does is copy other people's ideas' suggests not only a lack of creativity, but also a failure to predict and plan for the future (all examples of gaps between where we are and where we want to be).

It is at this point that analytical and creative problem-solving start to diverge. The analytical approach emphasizes the quantification of what is wrong with the current situation – lost output, reduced productivity, lost sales, and so on. The creative approach, on the other hand, is content to recognize that the current situation does not meet the wishes of the problem-owner and saves quantification until a later stage. With either approach, however, it will be necessary to compare the cost of alternative solutions with the cost of leaving the situation as it is, as we shall see later.

What has caused the problem?

This question is central to analytical problem-solving. A deviation from the norm means, by definition, that things were running smoothly, then something happened to disrupt them. An analysis of when the problem occurs, how often, under what circumstances and where, enables the problem to be pinpointed. Possible causes can then be identified and each one assessed to establish whether the effect resulting from it is consistent with the condition arising from the problem.

This analysis is far less important to the creative approach. In fact, those in favour of creative problem-solving would argue that defining the problem too narrowly automatically closes the door on solutions which, although they may not address the problem directly, offer wider improvements. Nevertheless, it is still helpful to find out why this problem is suddenly a priority for the problem-owner, as part of the background to it.

CASE STUDY

The owner-manager of a small garage in West London asked for help in solving a problem of incapable staff. An analytical approach identified that this was not a deviation from the norm. The staff had never been capable. Further questioning using the creative approach identified that this was an issue because the owner was considering retirement and wanted to hand over the business to someone who could run it at a profit, so that he could continue to draw dividends.

What are its longer-term consequences?

This question is helpful in determining:

- the urgency of the need for a solution
- whether the problem warrants a solution now or at all.

We can exemplify both points by considering the same hypothetical situation.

CASE STUDY

Imagine a light-engineering company manufacturing mild steel pressings. By monitoring the volume of waste product, it has identified a deviation from the norm in the shape of a growing number of rejects caused by the gradual wearing out of its machines. However, the company has also recognized that it has enough machine capacity to meet demand for the next five years, using quality control techniques to ensure customer satisfaction and assuming that the reject rate continues to increase in line with the current trends. It has also calculated that the cost of replacing its old machines would be significantly higher than the cost of lost production and tighter quality control over those five years.

Using creative problem-solving, the company has also established that, within five years, it would be well advised to get out of the metal pressings market, in view of declining demand and growing overseas competition. Where it wants to be is in the manufacture of electronic components, requiring totally different machinery.

In this example, it is clear that the company, whilst certainly having a problem, would be better off living with it for five years, at which point the problem will have changed beyond recognition.

We can draw a number of conclusions from this:

- Doing nothing can be a valid response to some problems.
- Such a decision can only be justified by a careful analysis of longer-term costs and consequences.
- Short-term solutions must take account of longer-term strategic direction.
- Solutions to today's problems may well not be relevant to tomorrow's problems.

Nevertheless, it would be dangerous to imply too much from these conclusions. A temptation to be avoided is that of ignoring small-scale tactical action to resolve a problem, in favour of waiting for a larger strategic initiative to mop it up along with several others. There are three reasons for avoiding this temptation:

- the potential cost and inconvenience of living with the problem
- the drawback, which was described in Chapter 8, that operational teams at the 'sharp end' of the business gain no practice in implementing change
- the fact that reliance on strategic change to bring about improvement means that change is always imposed on people from outside, rather than being a home-grown process.

It is for these reasons that the decision to tackle a problem or not should be based on an analysis of the consequences and on objective consideration of the outcomes of a strategic initiative, rather than wishful thinking.

To whom is it important?

This question relates to three separate categories of people:

- the problem-owner
- the authority-holder
- the solution-implementer.

The problem-owner

This is the person on whom the problem has the greatest impact, the one who is sufficiently dissatisfied with the present situation to be motivated to solve it.

Vincent Nolan recommends finding answers to five questions about that individual:

- Is the person willing to do something about it or just looking for sympathy?
- Is that person prepared to make a personal effort or are they expecting someone else to solve the problem for them?
- What is the problem-owner's power to act? What action are they empowered to take? What resources do they have available? What are the limits to the solutions they can implement?

- Is the problem-owner seeking a solution or proof that none exists? (with a consequent wish for sympathy, as above).

The authority-holder

This is the person with the authority and access to resources necessary for solving the problem. As we have already mentioned, the process of delegated decision-making and empowerment are making it increasingly likely that the problem-owner and the authority-holder will be one and the same person. However, two words of caution are necessary:

- Empowerment is a textbook philosophy. Whilst most organizations nowadays are committed to the idea of delegated authority, this is not always translated into action which makes it possible. The following case study provides a simple explanation.

CASE STUDY

The Premises Supervisor of Wolverhampton Training Centre is responsible for reception, catering and maintenance. The caretaker on site, who looks after minor repairs and also organizes tea, coffee and sandwiches for delegates, reports to her. However, she cannot authorize petty cash expenditure over £25. As a result, the purchase of materials for repairs or of most replacement equipment (a couple of flipchart pads, for example) has to be referred to higher management for approval or a formal order.

It is therefore not unusual for a problem-owner to know exactly what needs to be done to solve the problem, but to be prevented from implementing the solution because the problem is causing no inconvenience to the person who can authorize the resources or expenditure needed to resolve it, who therefore does not see it as worth tackling.

- The 'jobsworth' response. I have used this title to describe a response to problems which was historically common in role cultures (see Chapter 4). It is the idea that problems are 'their' fault and that it is up to 'them' to solve them. 'They' may be the management or another team or department. The problem-owner is demonstrating some of the behaviours we described earlier:

- looking for sympathy rather than action
- expecting someone else to solve the problem
- subconsciously hoping for confirmation that a solution is impossible, thereby expecting sympathy and the opportunity to blame someone else.

We shall examine the question of what an ideal solution would look like a little later in this chapter. For the moment, it is worth stressing that the best antidote to the 'jobsworth' response is for the problem-owner to ask: NOT 'What should they do to solve this problem?' BUT RATHER 'What can I do to solve it?'

CASE STUDY

Relate (formerly the Marriage Guidance Council) offers a valuable piece of advice to couples who are struggling with incompatible expectations, attitudes or behaviour in their relationships. The advice is to recognize that one partner has neither the power nor the right to change the other. Instead, both partners should ask themselves: 'What can I change about myself which will resolve this problem?'

The solution-implementer

This is the person, or group of people, who will be responsible for taking the action to resolve the problem. The following recommendations should come as no surprise:

- Implementers should know the background to the problem, why it is a problem and what the solution is intended to achieve.
- The more they are involved in designing the solution, the more committed they will be.
- Implementers need access to suitable resources.

CASE STUDY

A food processing plant in Liverpool continued to use machines first introduced twenty years previously. The workforce was asked to suggest ways of improving morale and productivity. One group pointed to the machines they operated and explained forcefully that the only way they would keep them working was by using clothes-pegs, odd bolts, lengths of timber and cardboard boxes, which the management would see if only they bothered to come down from their ivory towers and look.

How would this look if the problem were resolved?

The answer to this question varies according to the problem-solving approach you are following. The analytical answer is straightforward: things have been restored to the status quo.

The creative answer requires considerably more effort. Vincent Nolan explains: 'To articulate the need in a really powerful way so that it becomes a magnet for new ideas and a real stimulus to our creative abilities, we have to re-learn how to wish for the impossible'.

Wishing for the impossible is not a normal management process! Nevertheless, a number of techniques exist to encourage the process:

- writing a 'vision of the future'. This involves writing a fantasy description of the way things would look if your operation were successful beyond your wildest expectations.
- wishing in picture form. A variation on the first technique, by which you imagine in visual form a perfect version of your operation and then analyse what makes it perfect.
- springboards. This involves using phrases like 'I wish we could ...', 'It would be so much better if ...', then recording the rest of the sentence and using it as a springboard to move on to more extravagant wishes.
- backwards/forwards planning. This technique starts with the problem as defined, and assumes a solution has been found. It then looks for additional benefits which would arise from that solution. For example: the original problem is how to speed up the processing of customer payments. If customer payments were processed faster, this would improve cash flow. So the problem becomes: how to improve cash flow. The benefit of improved cash flow would be more money available for investment. So the problem now becomes: how to make more money available for investment.

Of course, this technique can be carried to ridiculous extremes, such as where the problem becomes: how to make this organization more successful.

However, it is helpful to advance backwards/forwards planning to the point where it reaches natural boundaries: the limits of an operation, for example, or of a manager's authority.

What are the alternative solutions?

This is where our two approaches to problem-solving converge again. Regardless of whether you have a specifically defined problem derived from the analytical approach, or a loose definition based on the creative approach, you are most likely to come up with an effective solution if you have generated an extensive menu to choose from.

Idea generation can employ a wide range of methods. For example:

- brainstorming
- lateral thinking
- word association
- visualizing
- doodling.

The essence of any of these is to deliberately cast off the restraints of past experience ('we tried that before – it didn't work'), practicability ('they'd never allow it' or 'we haven't the resources') or even common sense ('that's a daft idea'). Instead, the first stage of idea generation is to let your thoughts and your imagination roam freely, discarding nothing, no matter how impossible it may appear.

Some of these methods can be used by an individual. However, idea generation is most powerful when used by a group, so that people can build on others' ideas, or use them as a springboard for their own.

The second stage of idea generation is to go back to the list of alternatives you have identified and weed out those which are not worth taking further. This may be because they are:

- illegal
- inconsistent with the organization's values
- dependent on resources or technology which the organization cannot obtain.

It is important, though, not to discard ideas too soon. It may be possible to adapt or combine them to develop a further alternative which is free from the disadvantages of the original idea.

How much would each cost?

This question is, in fact, shorthand for a much longer series of questions. To answer it requires accurate analysis of the following:

- What physical resources (staff, equipment, space) will each solution require?
- How much will those resources cost?
- What expertise will each solution require?
- Is it available in-house or will it need to be bought in?
- How much will that expertise cost?
- How long will implementation take?
- How much disruption will it involve?
- What will the disruption cost in terms of lost output, customer inconvenience, staff resistance?
- How much added value will each solution bring?
- How does that added value compare with the costs involved?

These are not calculations that can be made on the back of an envelope. Instead, they may need to involve the use of cost–benefit analysis, discounted cash flow (DCF) and certainly attention to the impact on both staff and customers (whether internal or external). Two overriding factors are particularly important:

- the need to approach each analysis in an objective way, resisting the temptation to take an optimistic view of apparently favourable solutions, whilst assuming the worst of solutions which are less attractive at first sight
- a recognition that any change initiative is likely to need more resources, take longer, involve more disruption and cost more than the planners anticipated.

This apparently cynical comment is invariably borne out by experience.

CASE STUDY

The dream of a road-link to France has inspired people in Britain since the successful conclusion of the Napoleonic wars. In 1987 Eurotunnel went to the market for funding to undertake the Channel Tunnel. The amount sought proved woefully inadequate. Eurotunnel has experienced:

- disputes with contractors
- death of workers, attributed to poor safety regulations
- changes of government
- a fire in the tunnel
- major cash flow difficulties on the part of the rail operator.

We do not know how much risk analysis Eurotunnel carried out, to determine what might go wrong and what the consequences would be. All we can say is that the risk analysis was significantly more optimistic than hindsight shows it should have been.

Which provides the best fit with the problem?

This question is closely related to the last one and also needs to be rephrased in greater detail. It is really asking: which alternative solution deals with most of the problem at the least cost?

Of course, there are two sides to this more detailed question. On the one hand, do the problem-owner and the authority-holder prefer a cheap, quick and dirty solution which deals with the worst result of the problem? Or are they prepared to resource a more complex, sophisticated and costly solution which eliminates the problem entirely and adds value elsewhere at the same time?

Our two approaches to problem-solving reveal different preferences at this stage. Analytical problem-solving results in a solution which addresses the root cause of the problem, but has no interest in spin-off benefits. Creative problem-solving, by contrast, is likely to come up with a large-scale solution which overcomes the problem, adds value elsewhere, but may well involve significant resources, disruption and cost.

How the organization defines 'best fit' will be a result of its culture and the environmental factors impacting on it. Using the descriptions from Chapter 4, a power culture will pour an unlimited quantity of resources into resolving a problem which senior managers are convinced is important. A task culture is committed to ideas, expertise and experimentation. It will favour interesting solutions which may lead to exciting consequences elsewhere (good or bad). A role culture is subject to rules, procedures and hierarchical controls. Solutions will be expected to resolve the problem, be cost-effective and not to create waves elsewhere in the organization.

Environmental fit relates primarily to the speed and discontinuity of external change. As we mentioned earlier, analytical problem-solving stems from a stable and relatively predictable era. In consequence, it results in solutions which are limited and focused. If your organization operates in a relatively stable environment – and does not envisage dramatic change – then limited, cost-effective solutions without implications are likely to be favoured. On the other hand, if your organization identifies with the writings of Tom Peters, John Naisbitt, Alvin Toffler or Charles Handy, and is seeing itself as subject to discontinuous economic, social, technological or competitive change, it is likely to be willing to support solutions which are far-reaching in scope and costly to implement.

Following the steps we have described, it is reasonably straightforward to solve problems in an organization whose culture is consistent with its environment. But what should an operations manager do in an organization where the culture and the environment are not in line with each other? There are two possibilities, neither of which is easy.

The first is to create a local culture which is genuinely consistent with the environment. This will result in an ongoing confrontation with the style, controls and procedures which apply in the rest of the organization, but will at least make your operation responsive to the environment which, ultimately, governs it.

The second is to undertake an education and transformation programme throughout the organization, in order to bring it in line with the environment. The success of this initiative will depend on the extent to which other managers and other departments have recognized the inconsistency between the culture of the organization and the reality of the organization.

How can it be implemented?

We gave most of the answers to this question in Chapter 8. It involves:

- flow-charting the activities involved
- calculating resources, costs and time-scales
- identifying and allocating responsibilities
- communicating reasons, standards and deadlines
- designing and implementing a monitoring and control system
- carrying out a risk analysis
- deciding 'what do we do if this or that goes wrong?'

In the previous step, you identified the best-fit solution. However, it is important to recognize that, even at this final stage, it may be necessary to revise your previous choice. This is the last opportunity to ask some searching questions:

- Is this really possible in the time?
- Are those costs realistic?
- Are these people really capable of delivering the results we need?
- Can we afford the risk?
- Can we afford the consequences if it does go wrong?

The answers to these questions may result in the choice of an alternative solution, or a change to:

- time-scale
- resources
- people
- contingency plans.

They may even result in a decision that it is preferable to remain with the current situation, because all of the alternatives are too risky.

Stage / Approach	Problem definition	Identification of causes	Analysis of consequences	Ideal solution	Idea generation	Cost and fit	Implementation
Creative	Loose	May limit creativity	Qualitative	Wish fulfilment	Unconstrained	Objective quantified	Planned calculated
Analytical	Tight	Essential	Quantitative	Status quo	Unconstrained	Objective quantified	Planned calculated

Figure 9.1   Approaches to problem-solving

Figure 9.1 highlights the differences and similarities between our two approaches to problem-solving at successive stages of the process.

FORCE-FIELD ANALYSIS

The concept of force-field analysis

The concept of force-field analysis was developed in the 1930s by management scientist Kurt Lewin, in an attempt to explain why organizations found the successful implementation of change so difficult. Lewin started from the premise that the purpose of change is to bring about improvement. In theory, therefore, change should be welcome. But his research showed – and our own experience confirms – that change is often resisted.

Lewin suggested that this is because there are two sets of opposing forces at work in an organization – driving forces and restraining forces. He argued that change fails to take place when the two sets of forces are equally balanced. His diagram representing force-field analysis is shown in Figure 9.2.

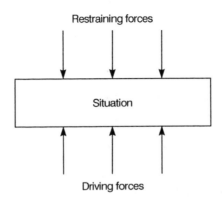

Figure 9.2   Force-field analysis

Driving forces are those which promote change. Restraining forces are those which maintain the status quo. While these two sets of forces remain equal and opposite, the situation remains in balance; no change takes place. A practical example will illustrate this effect.

CASE STUDY

When Sir Michael Edwardes took over as boss of British Leyland, the company was losing sales and market share, becoming increasingly uncompetitive and risked going out of business. He identified an obvious and urgent need for change if the company was to survive. However, it took several years of effort and struggle to bring those changes about. The driving forces for change included:

- threat of withdrawal of government subsidy if improvements did not take place
- declining profitability
- superior competitor products
- Michael Edwardes's own dynamism
- loss of customer loyalty.

The restraining forces, however, were equally real and powerful:

- an excessively strong union
- restrictive practices
- deep worker distrust of management
- weak and often incompetent management
- lack of money for investment.

A force-field analysis of British Leyland at the time would have looked like the diagram in Figure 9.3.

Force-field analysis as an aid to change

The first stage in using force-field analysis is to identify all the forces at work on an organization. These may be external or environmental forces such as those described in Chapters 2 and 4 of this book. It is significant that, in the British Leyland example, three of the driving forces for change (threatened loss of subsidy, superior competition, loss of customer loyalty) are all external forces. Or the forces may be internal, as are all the remainder in the British Leyland case.

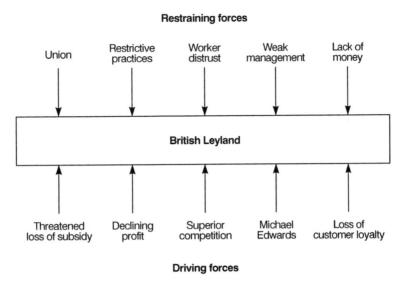

Figure 9.3   Force-field analysis of British Leyland

Having identified all the forces and categorized them as driving or restraining forces, it is then possible to work out ways of enabling change through one of two overarching processes.

Increasing the driving forces

This may involve increasing the power of existing forces, or adding others to tip the balance in favour of change.

Of course, it is not strictly possible to increase the power of external forces – they are as they are and, by definition, the organization has no influence over environmental factors. Nevertheless, external forces can be made more powerful by initiatives to ensure that the members of an organization are aware and convinced of their existence, their impact and their implications; in other words, the threat involved in ignoring them.

It is easier to increase the power of internal forces. Managers can shout louder, staff can be sacked or laid off, new technology can be introduced without consultation.

Increasing the driving forces is often described as a 'push' strategy for managing change. However, Lewin's original research and later studies all show that push strategies are less effective and more prone to failure than the alternative. Typically, this is because people, when pushed, have a natural tendency to push back. So the restraining forces increase to balance out the increased driving forces.

Reducing the restraining forces

This, as you would expect, is alternatively known as a 'pull' strategy for managing change. It involves identifying and reducing or eliminating the causes of resistance.

In the British Leyland case, Michael Edwardes set out to reduce resistance by:

- confronting the unions. This was not painless. It resulted in several strikes and carried significant costs in lost production. Ultimately, however, the company achieved a management–union relationship based on partnership rather than mutual antagonism.
- removing weak managers. Again, this was not without pain. Several managers lost their jobs. However, the argument was that workers could not be expected to trust incompetent managers and that managers who were not strong enough to do the jobs they were paid for did not deserve to have them.
- increasing worker participation. Edwardes decided to involve shop-floor workers more in decision-making, as a way both of increasing their trust and of improving decisions. The following case study illustrates his approach.

CASE STUDY

Soon after joining, Edwardes visited the Longbridge factory. He walked down the production-line and stopped to talk to one of the hands. He asked him: 'What's going wrong here?'

The hand replied: 'I'm not going to tell you in front of this lot. But come back at 8 tomorrow morning. I'll tell you then.'

Edwardes came back the following morning and talked privately to the hand for an hour. The news spread through the business that here at last was a manager who kept his word and was willing to listen to the workers.

INVOLVING OTHERS

QUESTION

Based on what you have read so far, who do you think should be involved in managing change?

Our answer would include three categories of people:

- the problem-owner
- the authority-holder
- the solution-implementers.

We looked briefly at each of these categories earlier in the chapter.

The problem-owner

In the context of managing change, this may not be quite the right title. Nevertheless, as change is intended to bring improvement and improvement is only necessary when things are not going as well as they should be, managing change and solving problems are closely linked.

It may seem unnecessary to include the problem-owner in our classification of people to be involved. Surely their involvement is so obvious as not to be worth mentioning? Surprisingly often, though, they are not involved. In a hierarchical organization, or one which takes a paternalistic view of its staff, decisions are taken to implement change (for example, in the form of changed procedures or documentation, or new operating practices) without consulting those who will be most directly affected by the change. The implied message is: 'This will be good for you whether you like it or not.'

That message is a powerful way of increasing restraining forces against change by building fear or resentment. Any change initiative, however desirable, must be acceptable to the problem-owner if it is going to succeed.

CASE STUDY

When the British government, in response to the BSE crisis, passed a new law banning the sale of beef on the bone, many retailers ignored it and continued to sell T-bone steaks and oxtail. Customers – the problem-owners in this case – rejected the argument that the new law was good for them, preferring instead to be left to make their own decisions about whether they wanted the product.

The authority-holder

We could have said, quite simply, 'the boss'. Authority figures have two important roles to play in managing change. First, they will often need to authorize the intended change and to make resources available to support it. It is therefore essential for them to know the nature of the change, its benefits and its implications.

Secondly, the authority of the boss is often a crucial driving force for change. Knowing that the boss is in favour, provided he or she has the respect of the workforce, and hearing from him or her the reasons for and the thinking behind the change, does much both to make the need for change convincing and to lessen the resistance.

The solution-implementers

We have already used the buzz words which relate to this group:

- consultation
- participation
- gaining commitment
- the need for communication.

These apply to managing change just as much as they do to any other aspect of decision-making.

COMPETENCE SELF-ASSESSMENT

1   What changes have recently taken place in the operation for which you are responsible?

2   Based on the ten questions of problem-solving, how well were they managed?

3   Does your organization favour analytical or creative problem-solving?

4   Is its preferred approach consistent with the environment in which it operates?

5   What changes would you like to make to achieve your vision for your operation?

6   What driving forces promote those changes?

7   What are the restraining forces in opposition to them?

8   Are the members of your team in favour of change? How could you increase their support?

9   What is your attitude to change? Why?

10   What more could you do to increase your own manager's support for and commitment to change?

10 Managing people

'At last!' exclaimed our personnel officer. 'A chapter on people – and about time, too, if I may say so. How this book expects anyone to manage operations effectively without being able to manage people, I cannot imagine. Motivation, communication, empowerment, involvement, training, performance appraisal – they're all central to a modern manager's job. It's going to be a struggle to fit all of those into a single chapter, I can tell you.'

'Now hold on', said the marketing manager. 'This isn't a human resources textbook. It's not fair for you to expect comprehensive coverage of your subject. I'd argue that customer service is central to the modern manager's job, too – but this isn't a marketing textbook, either. So, we've only had a few references to marketing principles. In the same way, accounting has only cropped up a few times. But I bet our beloved accountant would argue that a good manager has to be able to use accounting techniques as well.'

'That's right', agreed the production supervisor. 'This book is about operations management. As I see it, people are resources to be used in transforming inputs into outputs. Important resources, of course. But no more important than machinery, equipment, space, raw materials, systems and procedures. I certainly want to learn more about managing people – but only to help me be a more effective operations manager. The fancy stuff can wait for a different book!'

Those early exchanges put this chapter's coverage of people management into context and into proportion. The subject of operations management incorporates ideas and techniques from a wide range of management disciplines:

- marketing and particularly customer service
- quality management
- production scheduling
- stock control and stock management
- capacity management
- strategic planning
- objective setting
- output and performance management
- problem-solving and decision-making
- managing health and safety
- financial accounting.

It is therefore important to recognize that operations management is a generalist, rather than an expert, function. That comment is not intended to belittle the function. Rather, it is an acknowledgement of the old adage that: 'Experts are people who know more and more about less and less, to the point where they know almost everything about nothing at all.'

Consequently, this chapter is consistent with the wishes of the production supervisor. It is intended to deal with those aspects of the management of people which have an impact on operations management, but without going into exhaustive detail.

Nevertheless, we would agree with the personnel officer that people management is a wide-ranging topic. Therefore, the chapter has a lot of ground to cover, particularly in view of the fact that, in the context of operations management, the people to be managed are not just subordinates, but colleagues and bosses as well.

In order to cover this ground, the chapter is split into the following sections:

Managing subordinates

- assessing ability and potential
- communication and involvement
- empowerment
- developing capability.

Managing colleagues

- consulting and informing
- developing confidence.

Managing the boss

- representing your people
- upward communication
- seeking direction.

MANAGING SUBORDINATES

The way a manager manages subordinates is dependent on three factors:

- personality and personal style
- the culture of the organization
- the nature of the work.

Some managers feel more comfortable giving orders, in the expectation that subordinates will follow them. This may be the result of personality, or of the work environment in which managers have learnt their trade.

Tannenbaum and Schmidt, two American psychologists, developed a model of the use of authority by managers (see Figure 10.1).

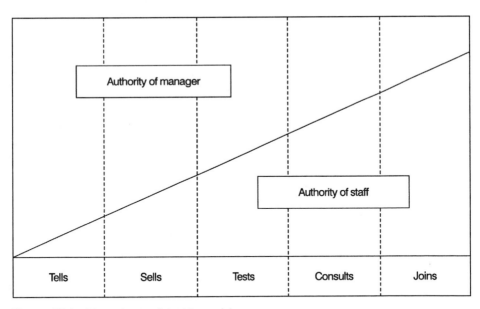

Figure 10.1   Tannenbaum–Schmidt model

The Tannenbaum–Schmidt continuum of decision-making is based on the premise that any management decision requires a finite amount of input. The more input from the manager to a decision (in the shape of authority), the less scope there is for input from staff (in the shape of involvement in the decision).

This model incorporates five different management styles of decision-making, as described below:

- In the *telling* style, the manager identifies the problem or the need for a decision, considers alternatives and chooses one of them. Staff are informed of the decision and instructed to implement it. Their thoughts or feelings are not taken into account.

- In the *selling* style, the manager identifies the problem and decides on a solution. However, there is a recognition that the decision may meet with resistance from staff affected by it. In order to deal with that resistance, the decision is not simply announced. Instead, the manager makes an effort to sell it by promoting the benefits the decision will bring to staff.

- In the *testing* style, the manager reaches a tentative decision. But, before that decision is finalized, the manager presents it and tests its viability by judging staff reactions. The manager still reserves the right to take the final decision.

- In the *consulting* style, the manager identifies the problem and presents it to staff for suggested solutions. The manager evaluates staff suggestions and chooses the one which seems most promising.

- In the *joining* style, the manager identifies the problem, but then passes it to staff to analyse and decide on a solution. The manager may join the staff in this decision-making process, but the group is given the right to make the final decision and the manager agrees to implement it.

QUESTION

Which of these decision-making styles is most natural for you?

There is no right answer to this question. Your style will have developed as a result of what is natural for you on one hand, and the expectations of the organizations in which you have worked on the other.

Organizations have a marked tendency to recruit and develop both managers and staff in their own image. So, for example, organizations with an autocratic style will develop managers who are comfortable giving orders and recruit staff who are happy obeying them.

In the 1980s, Do-It-All, the chain of DIY superstores, had a culture of unquestioning obedience. In the course of a training event, one manager remarked: 'If I tell a member of my staff to jump, the only question I expect is "How high?"'

So, where does organizational style come from? In part from history, but also in large part from the nature of the work. Organizations that depend on routine, consistent work tend to have a style which demands obedience to instructions. At the other extreme, organizations that depend on creativity and innovation favour a consultative style which expects and welcomes staff who question routines, procedures and instructions.

However, this apparently universal picture is overly simplistic. Consider the following example.

At first glance, the military is a classic example of an organization which demands obedience without question. In fact, the reality in the British Army is significantly different. The unpredictability of modern battle makes it essential for soldiers at all levels to be able to make decisions for themselves. Consequently, their training emphasizes situation analysis, solution generation and the evaluation of alternatives.

At the same time, there are still situations which demand automatic obedience. As a senior officer recently remarked: 'We expect our personnel to think for themselves. But they are all dependent on each other. So there will always be life-threatening situations where they need to follow orders without question.'

The sections on managing subordinates which follow therefore seek to take account of personal style, the expectations of your organization, as well as best current practice and the demands of operational effectiveness.

Assessing ability and potential

In earlier chapters of this book, we have referred to the techniques and benefits of performance appraisal. In summary, the process involves:

- reviewing past performance against objectives
- identifying strengths and weaknesses of performance
- agreeing future objectives
- agreeing any training or support needed to achieve future objectives and deal with past weaknesses.

Performance is then monitored informally on an ongoing basis and discussed with the subordinate, in preparation for the next formal appraisal review or interview.

The way you approach performance appraisal will depend on:

- the system in place in your organization
- your view of what will be required of your operation in future and the operating procedures you expect your staff to use.

There are two ways of handling any appraisal system, one unproductive and the other productive. The way you are used to is likely to depend on the culture of the organization in which you work.

The unproductive approach to appraisal involves the mechanical completion of the documentation any such system demands. The personnel or human resource department sends out the papers and sets deadlines for their return. Managers tick boxes, award grades, write out objectives largely based on those set for the last period and agree training in a discussion which mainly takes the form of: 'Here's the brochure. Is there anything you fancy doing in that list?'

CASE STUDY

A trainee from a major high street retailer attended an in-house retail marketing course. When asked why he was there and what he wanted to get out of the course, his answer was: 'Well, I've done everything on the list except marketing and retail finance – and I wasn't keen on doing the finance.'

Of course, that approach, as we pointed out in our earlier chapter, sends some important messages to the workforce. They include:

- We don't really value our own people.
- We're not interested in developing skills.
- Managing people just involves going through the motions.

In a minority of cases, the system is so designed that there is no alternative to this approach. Deadlines for turning round the paperwork are so tight that the time is simply not available for managers and subordinates to prepare for and conduct the necessary interviews in a meaningful way.

More often, however, the system is abused because managers and subordinates have failed to recognize the potential benefits it offers. The benefits of an effective appraisal system are:

- The workforce feels valued.
- Individuals gain knowledge, skills and experience which are relevant both to their current jobs and to future careers.
- Performance throughout the organization improves.
- Output increases.
- Errors, costs and waste decrease.

The productive use of appraisal involves:

- Giving honest, accurate, but constructive feedback on past performance.
- Setting objectives which are stretching but achievable.
- Arranging training (not just formal courses but also coaching, self-study, guided experience) which is relevant to the individual.
- Regarding appraisal as a continuous approach, not just a matter of completing the forms once or twice a year.

The linkage between operational needs and appraisal is an important one. It is also a two-way process. Earlier in this book we looked in detail at continuous improvement and managing change. Changes to required outputs – their nature or quantity – will depend partly for their success on your subordinates' ability to deliver them. Consequently, you need to ask yourself:

- Are my staff currently capable of producing more, better or otherwise different outputs?
- If not, do they have the potential to learn?
- If not, can these changes to output be achieved without demanding more from my staff?
- If not, are these changes necessary or even possible?
- If so, will I need a new workforce?

Communication and involvement

At an organizational level, attitudes to communication and involvement will depend heavily on culture. Using the descriptions introduced in Chapter 4:

- Power cultures keep information at the centre. Communication takes the form of instructions. Involvement is limited to power-holders.
- Task cultures are open. Information and expertise are shared within teams, although there is a tendency to take little or no interest in what other, unrelated teams are doing. Teams will be heavily involved in decisions affecting their own operations. The principal communication problem is likely to be persuading people to take notice of organizational matters which do not affect them directly.
- Role cultures will have a formal, top-down communication structure. There will be formal communications systems and procedures in place (management briefings, newsletters, noticeboards, electronic mail). Involvement in decisions will be limited, although bureaucracies are increasingly using formal task groups or working parties to increase participation.
- Person cultures will see little need for regular communication, since each individual is really running a separate operation. However, decisions which are necessary (for example, upgrading the switchboard, hiring another member of support staff) will be taken jointly. This is, first, because in most person cultures any such decision will have a financial impact on everyone and, secondly, because members of a person culture tend to be distrustful of others' ability to take sound decisions.

It is unlikely that you will be able to have much influence on the overall culture of your organization. Nevertheless, in cultures where information is not fully available, it will be helpful to identify those who hold it and to establish relationships with them which will enable you to keep yourself informed.

As far as your own operation is concerned, you have far greater control. As we have pointed out elsewhere in this book, communication increases motivation and the more people are involved in decisions, the more committed they will be to them. The way you communicate is also significant. Regular team and face-to-face briefings are more effective than reliance on the printed word or electronic mail, although some communication will be complex enough to benefit from paper back-up. Also, involving people in decisions should not just happen all of a sudden. Staff involvement in decision-making needs to be a way of life, otherwise they will neither expect, welcome or have the mental agility to cope with it.

Empowerment

Empowerment has been a consistent theme of this book. It involves giving your staff ownership of the work they do, together with the responsibility and authority to carry it out and to seek and implement changes and improvements. Many of the trends and developments in the structure and management of organizations, which were discussed in Chapter 2, are based on the twin foundations of empowerment and delegated responsibility.

However, it would be misleading to claim that empowerment is a painless process, either for managers or for their subordinates. Managers are often appointed because of their technical expertise. They take a pride in their work and rightly set high quality standards. They therefore often suffer from a real concern that the delegation of tasks historically done by the manager will result in a decline in quality. Unfortunately, this view leads to a vicious circle. Because managers fail to delegate, subordinates do not have the opportunity to learn. Because they do not learn, they cannot do the task. Consequently, managers are afraid to delegate to subordinates whom they know lack the necessary skills.

Successful empowerment therefore brings together several techniques and approaches mentioned elsewhere in this book. It depends on:

- a willingness to take risks (at least in the first place)
- careful and detailed monitoring of quality and results (which can be reduced over time)
- the provision of relevant training
- the availability of the manager so that the subordinate can consult and check understanding
- clear communication of the task and performance standards
- systems for the subordinate to monitor and control their own performance against those standards.

It should be noted that empowerment is not a process of suddenly deciding that your subordinates are capable of more than you used to think, dumping extra tasks on them and walking away. That is abdication, not delegation! Instead, it involves the communication, support and monitoring just summarized.

A final word of warning. Empowerment brings short-term pain for long-term gain. In the short term, it involves extra time, extra effort and extra fear that things will go wrong. In the long term, it will:

- free you to spend more time on genuinely managerial work
- develop your staff
- enrich their jobs

- contribute to the organization's human resource planning by increasing skill levels
- increase job satisfaction.

CASE STUDY

A small manufacturing business on the outskirts of Birmingham had three directors. They typically worked twelve-hour days, often at weekends as well. Despite their efforts, profits were falling and staff turnover was high. A larger competitor bought them out. The competitor had recognized that the directors were 'busy fools' – spending their time doing day-to-day tasks which could have been delegated, but paying no attention to long-term planning, developing markets or financial strategy. Staff were leaving out of boredom.

Developing capability

In an operational context, developing the capability of your staff is no less and no more than ensuring you have the human resources you need to carry out effectively the activities which make up the operation for which you are responsible. It is a far more limited process than the one you will see described in a textbook on staff development, which will look beyond the needs of the current job to examine aspects of career planning and long-term personal development, sometimes even outside the scope of the present employer's business.

The process of developing operational capability involves:

- careful analysis of each individual's job to determine the activities which constitute it
- a prediction of changes to the operation, to identify their impact on the nature of individual jobs
- the identification of the skills and knowledge needed to carry out the activities which make up the job, both now and in the foreseeable future
- a comparison between skills and knowledge required and those possessed by the jobholder
- the design and implementation of a remedial programme to create a match between skills and knowledge required and those possessed
- monitoring performance after the programme to ensure that the match has been achieved and that new skills and knowledge are being applied successfully.

- What benefits will the change bring? What quantifiable performance improvement will the change bring? If the benefits are purely qualitative, why are they worth the effort? If the change requires investment or brings drawbacks, how do these equate with the predicted improvements?
- How will you measure the improvement? It is rare nowadays that you will be allowed to make changes without measuring their effect. So how will you do this? And how will you know if they have succeeded?
- How will your boss know it has worked? Unless your boss is prepared to trust you absolutely, you will need to be able to show evidence of success. Will current performance measurement provide that evidence, or will you need a different method of performance feedback? Will the evidence come automatically and visibly, or will you need to present it personally?

Remember, too, that your boss should know that the suggested change or improvement has come from your staff. Not only will this demonstrate your ability as a manager to involve your staff in positive action, it will also enable your boss to raise meaningful questions when visiting your operation.

Upward communication

We have already referred to 'no surprises' as a central theme of effective management. You may also know from your own experience how easy it is for a manager to become separated from what is happening on the shop floor. Consequently, part of your responsibility to your boss is to provide information about what is happening in your operation. This may relate to:

- changes in your team
- the performance of the team or of individual team members
- problems you are facing
- the success of initiatives
- reasons for any deviations from performance standards.

Such information needs to be carefully considered before you share it. Ask yourself:

- Is this important enough to mention?
- How much detail does the boss need?

The remedial programme may take the form of:

- external training course (although it is important to ensure that its content is genuinely consistent with the individual's needs and that the quality of delivery is adequate)
- coaching from the manager
- side-by-side training from a more experienced colleague (who must, though, have the technical knowledge and skills required, as well as the ability to transfer them)
- self-study (textbooks, Open Learning, relevant professional articles)
- guided experience (made up of introductory coaching or training, followed by on-the-job practice and review).

As we pointed out earlier, it is a popular misconception to view training and development as outside activities for which the personnel or training function is responsible. Those functions may have an advisory or administrative role, but operations managers are as much responsible for the knowledge and skills of their staff as they are for ensuring the availability of raw materials or the regular maintenance of production machinery.

MANAGING COLLEAGUES

Earlier in this book, we referred to operations management as a horizontal process, with different teams, sections and departments in the organization all representing links in the supply chain, either as customers, suppliers or both. That is the context into which these next two sections fit. Managing colleagues means regular contact with them to ensure that:

- they know your needs and expectations of them, if you are the customer
- you know their needs and expectations of you, if you are the supplier
- or both, if you fit into both categories, as we explained in Chapter 4.

It also means keeping yourself and them up to date with developments and anticipated changes, so that these can be planned for. It finally means ensuring their confidence in your and your staff's technical or professional competence.

Consulting and informing

If your organization follows the total quality management procedures described earlier in this book, you should have a clear specification of your customers' requirements, set out in language they can identify with. If not, regular meetings with them will enable you or one of your team to draw up such a specification. This will enable you to determine what their needs are and to track how effectively those needs are being met. This should be an ongoing process, since one of the biggest traps for any operation providing customer service is to assume that what customers want now is what they have wanted in the past. Quantities, quality, speed of output and priorities can and will all change. When you know and have prioritized your customers' requirements, this may well result in your changing the activities you undertake to meet them. Again, it is a mistake to make those changes without consulting your customers. Use your regular meetings to find out:

- Will planned changes result in products and services which satisfy their requirements?
- Are those requirements sufficiently important to the customer to require revisions to your plans?

Similar meetings with your suppliers will enable you to:

- communicate to them your requirements and how well they are currently being met
- recommend improvements to the service you are currently receiving
- notify future changes to your requirements and their implications for suppliers' activities.

Meetings with customers and suppliers provide a valuable forum for feedback on performance against standards. However, as we have mentioned elsewhere, they should be regarded as joint problem-solving or continuous improvement activities; not as opportunities to criticize, lay blame or put down.

Developing confidence

One of the manager's key roles with regard to staff is to act as their ambassador. However, it is tempting to overlook this role and, instead, to play the hero by taking personal credit for successes whilst blaming your staff for failure. Instead, when meeting with colleagues, it is important to emphasize the ability and competence of your staff, building trust in them and giving them due credit for the quality and output of your operation. This approach is a far more accurate reflection of a manager's responsibility for staff. After all, if you have recruited, appraised, trained, consulted and communicated with them – and they are still not doing the job effectively – is that not likely to indicate that you, rather than they, are at fault?

MANAGING THE BOSS

The principle of empowerment and delegated responsibility may, at first give the impression that the importance of the boss has been reduced. T not, in fact, the case. Instead, the boss's role is different, not smaller.

Think back to what was said earlier about managing subordinates. It suggested that, in an ideal environment, the boss:

- informs and consults
- monitors performance
- advises and supports.

It is these activities which you should expect from your own boss. Howe there is a lot you can do to encourage them.

Representing your people

In several places in this book, I have stressed the value of seeking suggestion and recommendations from your staff for changes or improvements to th operation you manage. However, I have also pointed out that their implementa tion, even if desirable, may well be outside the limits of your authority. In tha case, you will need to seek authorization from your boss. But before doing so ask yourself the following questions:

- Is this initiative genuinely more than I can implement? Limits of authority can be viewed in two ways. From one viewpoint, they specify what you are entitled to do. Seen in that way, any action which is not specifically mentioned is outside your authority. And that is certainly limiting, since whoever drew them up is unlikely to have considered every possible action open to you. Alternatively, limits of authority can be viewed as specifying those things which you are not entitled to do. From that viewpoint, anything which is not specifically excluded is allowed. That gives you much wider scope!
- What is the evidence that change is desirable? If, having reviewed your limits of authority, you are still certain that you need permission from your boss, make sure that change can be justified. In other words: in what ways is your operation not meeting the performance standards set for it? Alternatively: in what ways are current practices, systems or procedures leading to frustration or demotivation amongst your staff?

- What are the wider implications of what I am about to share?
- What suggestions do I have for dealing with those implications?

Remember that upward communication is an updating process. It should not involve off-loading problems and decisions which are rightly yours onto your boss's shoulders.

Seeking direction

Chapters 2 and 7 explained the importance of operational objectives being derived from and contributing to the achievement of corporate goals. I have also described an ideal system of cascade briefing, whereby everybody in the organization is informed about corporate goals and how their work contributes to them. However, it would be unrealistic to expect that the ideal always applies! As a result, you may well find yourself in a position where you will need to know from your boss:

- where the organization is going
- what goals and objectives have been set for your boss
- how your operation is expected to contribute to them.

Of course, this information should be reaching you automatically but, in an imperfect world, there may be times when you will need to ask for it.

You may also need to ask for guidance when tackling problems in your operation. These may be:

- staff problems
- customer problems
- equipment problems
- input problems
- systems problems
- output problems.

However, remember our warning against using your boss as a dumping ground for problems you cannot be bothered to solve for yourself. Instead, make sure you have considered in advance:

- Is there any need to involve the boss? For example, does the problem have cross-functional or organizational implications?
- If so, what alternative solutions can I suggest?

You will get a more positive response if you can offer solutions as well as problems:

- What will be the consequences of my various suggested solutions?
- What inputs do I want from the boss?

These may be information ('What budget is available?') or support ('I need a temporary member of staff') or advice ('Tell me about Fred, I need some help from him but you know him better than I do').

Fundamental to these three ways of managing the boss is the need for regular meetings, briefings and communication. As you will remember from the description of centralized control in Chapter 2, a major drawback is that management becomes divorced from reality. This section has suggested some ways of keeping the boss out of the ivory tower!

COMPETENCE SELF-ASSESSMENT

1   How consistent is your personal style with the culture of your organization?

2   What would you prefer your style to be and how would you achieve it?

3   How effective is performance appraisal in your organization? How could it be improved?

4   What could you do to make more productive use of the appraisal process for your staff?

5   How could you improve communication within your team?

6   What more could you do to delegate decisions to your team? How could you ensure the success of that increased delegation?

7   What more could you do to develop the capability of your staff?

8   How could you improve communication with internal customers and suppliers?

9   How could you make better use of your boss to improve the performance of your operation?

10 What further information does your boss need that you do not currently provide?

Index

Printed in the United Kingdom
by Lightning Source UK Ltd.
111460UKS00001B/130